Homebre

Stout and Porter

Clive La Pensée
& Roger Protz

The authentic history of two global beer styles:

Recipes from the past made ready for you to brew at home.

Homebrew Classics
Stout and Porter

Authors: Clive La Pensée and Roger Protz

Cover design by Rob Howells

Cover photography by Thomas Dobbie

Printed by Wyndeham Gait, UK

Published by CAMRA, The Campaign for Real Ale, 230 Hatfield Road, St. Albans, Herts AL1 4LW

Managing Editor: Mark Webb, mark-webb@msn.com

© CAMRA Ltd 2003

ISBN 1-85249-130-2

CONTENTS

Introduction

This is a new kind of book for beer enthusiasts. Between its covers you will find a wealth of information about the particular brewing styles of two famous names in the history of beer: Stout and Porter. You will also find recipes and instructions to help you brew your own Stouts and Porters, with as much authenticity and/or creativity that you wish to employ.

Roger Protz takes us to the late 1600s, early 1700s, in the London streets where Porter was possibly born. What were the pubs like in those days? What did they have in their cellars and on their bars? What exactly was the mixture they served up to their customers? Were new beer styles the result of customer choice or advances in brewing technology?

For the story of Stout, it's off to Ireland, where the great names of Irish brewing, such as Guinness, Beamish and Murphy, are part of the tale of what is now a popular drink throughout the world.

Clive La Pensée provides the detail, the authentic recipes, the graft of brewing Stout and Porter. Homebrewers will find the ingredients, temperatures and timings that produced, and now reproduce, Stouts and Porters in their historic, authentic versions. His recipes are like the notes of a detective on the trail of a missing person. Reading them, and brewing with them, makes you part of the story.

Welcome to a new kind of book – the Homebrew Classics. Look out for other titles in the series on India Pale Ale, Lager, Mild, Bitter, and other famous beer styles.

Through a Glass Darkly

'Open two bottles of Stout, Jack,' said Mr O'Connor. 'How can I?' said the old man, 'when there's no corkscrew?' 'Wait now, wait now!' said Mr Henby, getting up quickly. 'Did you ever see this little trick?' He took two bottles of Stout from the table and, carrying them to the fire, put them on the hob. The he sat down again by the fire and took another drink from his bottle...In a few minutes an apologetic 'Pok!' was heard as the cork flew out of Mr Lyons' bottle. Mr Lyons jumped off the table, went to the fire, took his bottle and carried it to the table.

James Joyce, Ivy Day in the Committee Room,
from Dubliners, 1914.

Porter is a disputatious beer. Sit a group of brewers, or beer writer, or beer aficionados down in a tavern or bar to discuss India Pale Ale or Pilsner and lively but friendly discourse will ensue. But mention the dread word 'Porter' and tempers will rise and tables will start to be thumped. There are as many theories about the origins of Porter – its appearance, its taste, and even its name – as there are versions of the beer style brewed today. A small industry has developed among some beer writers as they attempt to create ever more fanciful notions about the beer and its name. This contribution to the debate prefers to deal with fact rather than fantasy.

The search for the origins of Porter and Stout begins in London at the turn of the eighteenth century. London then was developing from a series of loosely connected villages and small towns into the world's greatest city. Land enclosures had driven vast numbers of impoverished rural people into London and other urban areas. The consumption of beer rose rapidly to both refresh people engaged in heavy manual labour, and to offer some solace to the miserable lives of the urban poor.

To keep pace with consumption, brewing changed drastically. Commercial or 'common' brewers sprang up to supply inns, taverns and alehouses (the 'public house' did not exist until Victorian times) as well as passing trade. Brewing in inns and alehouses, once the main source of beer supply, went into rapid decline.

Brewing was encouraged by governments of the time as beer was seen as a healthy alternative to gin drinking, which was literally killing men, women and children: 'Drunk for a penny, dead drunk for tuppence' was the morbid sign outside a Southwark gin shop. Hogarth's savage portrait of the depravities of Gin Lane and the rosy-cheeked wassail in Beer Street produced a profound effect. Taxes on distilling sent the price of gin soaring and people turned to beer.

Nevertheless, the way in which beer itself was taxed played a part in the switch to a new type of ale that eventually became known as Porter. For centuries barley malt had been cured or 'kilned' over wood fires. The malt was brown and, as a result, beers in all countries were dark in colour. Once coal was used as fuel, brewers found they could control their kilns more easily as coal did not flare and scorch the malt, as wood frequently did. They also found that pale malt contained higher levels of starch and enzymes than brown malt. It is the action of enzymes on starch that produces fermentable brewing sugars, and pale malt produced ten per cent more sugary 'extract' than brown. As a result, more alcohol could be made from smaller amounts of malt. It was an important commercial consideration.

But there was a problem: coal was taxed, while wood was not, and coal fires gave off noxious gases that could infect the malt. The burning of coal was also restricted in urban areas because of the fogs it created. The use of pale malt did not become widespread until coke was developed as a bi-product of coal.

Pale beer was therefore very expensive. It was made by country brewers, men of power and wealth, who sold it to London brewers at a considerable profit. The same country brewers also bought fresh Brown Beer from London and matured it for many months in great oak tuns or vats. London brewers, based in inns or cramped commercial sites, did not have the space to build large tuns in which to store beer. Beer was matured in this manner as brewing was a seasonal activity. It was suspended during the summer as fermentation could not be controlled, and was ruined by both high ambient temperature and wild yeasts in the atmosphere.

Beers that were not matured, such as young London brown ale, had rough off-flavours and had to be blended with older beer to make them palatable. Mature or 'stale' beer was sold to London brewers at enormous profit.

The London brewers had no choice but to buy expensive pale and stale beers from the country brewers as their customers demanded a popular beer called 'three threads'. The name was a corruption of 'three thirds' as publicans had to mix beers from three different casks in their cellars: pale or uppenny (an indication of the high price of the style), young brown ale and mature stale. During its long maturation in unlined wooden casks, stale would be attacked by the wild yeast strain Brettanomyces – still used to ferment the gueuze and lambic beers of Belgium – giving it a sour, lactic aroma and flavour much admired by drinkers. Contrary to all the myths and legends about the style, it was these blended 'three threads' beers that were the first Porters, a mix of ales brewed in both London and the surrounding countryside. A London style of Porter followed. It was known at first as 'entire butt' or just entire. Both three threads and entire acquired the nickname of Porter but the two styles existed side by side for most of the eighteenth century. An engraving in the Whitbread Archive shows a pub advertising Whitbread London Porter and Whitbread & Co. Entire.

It is often said that a London brewer by the name of Ralph Harwood 'invented' the drink we know as Porter. Harwood without doubt brewed an entire butt beer and was almost certainly the first to do so. But to say he invented a style is to accept the big bang theory of brewing. Entire butt developed out of three threads and it did so partly because Harwood's customers tired of mixing beers in their cellars and also from the acute commercial desire of London brewers to break the stranglehold of the country brewers.

The first effort involved a brown ale made from wood-kilned malt with a high level of hops. Both malt and hops were taxed at the time but the duty on hops was lower than for malt. As a result the London brewers could make a bitter beer that was cheaper and far more profitable than three threads. But the beer went off quickly and, according to a contemporary writer, a former brewer who used the pen name of Obadiah Poundage, drinkers missed the more complex flavours of three threads. They started to blend London brown ale with country-brewed pale and stale bought from 'ale drapers' shops supplied by the country brewers. It was the continuing grip of the country brewers that led to the development of entire butt.

Ralph Harwood seized the initiative in 1722 by brewing a beer that attempted to reproduce the aroma and taste of three threads. Harwood was born in 1681 and died in 1749. In the intervening years he became a brewer and, with his brother James, ran the Bell Brewhouse in Byde's Place off Shoreditch High Street in East London. Both Byde's Place and the brewhouse have long since disappeared and Harwood's role in the history of British brewing became no more than a footnote. His modest annual production of 21,000 barrels was outstripped by a new generation of commercial brewers who built vast sites dedicated to the production of Porter and Stout. Although the Bell Brewhouse no longer exists, one of the Shoreditch pubs it supplied, the Old Blue Last in Great Eastern Street, still stands. A motif on the exterior wall says it was the first pub to sell Porter, though what it sold was Harwood's entire butt. The name 'entire' came from the fact that beer reached the pubs Harwood supplied in one cask, instead of separate casks from which three threads was blended. There is no information about how Harwood brewed beer or about the malts he used. It is assumed that entire butt was an unblended beer made from a single brew or mash but it was possibly a mix of two or three beers, which were blended in the brewery for the convenience of the customers. Harwood would not have stored ale in vats for several months to produce stale and would have bought supplies from country brewers to give his entire butt beer the lactic tang demanded by drinkers. Possibly he brewed one beer in his brewhouse and then blended it with stale. One theory suggests that Harwood brewed entire by mistake when he was supplied with over-kilned dark malt. This is as fanciful as the notion that the first golden lager brewed in Pilsen was the result of pale rather than brown malt being delivered to the brewery. If the wrong malt arrives at a brewery it is sent back.

Clive La Pensee deals with the question of malt in great deal in his section of this book. Suffice it to say here that the taste and colour of Harwood's entire was probably the result of a new type of brown malt developed at the time. In his *Maltster's Guide*, published in 1860, Edward Skeate White describes in great detail how 'Porter malt' was made. It was similar to modern crystal malt – a stewed malt that is delivered to the brewer with the malt starches already turned to sugar inside the grain. Porter malt was a response to the demand for Porter and Stout in London, but it would not have been available when Harwood first brewed his Entire Butt. It is more likely that Harwood used a new type of 'high dried' brown malt that, as a result of careful kilning, contained a higher level of enzymes than conventional wood-kilned malt. This high dried brown malt would have given Harwood's entire a good colour and flavour, and would have enabled him to use less expensive pale malt.

It is often said that Harwood's entire butt was a sensation that took London by storm and changed the face of brewing overnight. In fact it took some time for entire and Porter beers to dominate the London market. Communication was poor, and most people were illiterate or semi-literate. News was disseminated from the pulpit rather than from newspapers, and it is not likely that parsons proclaimed the joys of Mr Harwood's new entire. Professor Richard Bradley *Guide to Gentleman Farmers and Housekeepers for Brewing the Finest Malt Liqueurs* published in 1727 did not mention Porter or entire, but he may have been unaware of developments in London. More surprisingly, the *London and Country Brewer*, first published in 1734, says that the most popular beers of the day were Stout Beer, Strong Brown Ale (known as Stitch) and common Brown Ale. The Stout would not have been the type of beer we know today: it was the generic name for the strongest or stoutest beer produced in a brewery. In his *Poem to Stella* in 1720, written in London two years before Ralph Harwood first made entire, the Irish poet and satirist Jonathan Swift referred to 'a pint of Stout'. When the brewing of Porter started to expand and some breweries concentrated solely on its production, the strongest Porters were dubbed 'Stout Porters'.

Twenty-four years after the first edition of the *London and Country Brewer*, H. Jackson *Essay on Bread* of 1758 recorded that 'beer, commonly called Porter, is become almost the universal cordial of the populace'.

One reason for the surge in sales of entire and Porter may have been a Parliamentary Act of 1742 to combat gin drinking. And the comparative cheapness of Porter compared to pale ale ('tuppenny') and new versions of brown ale made from lightly kilned amber malt would have increased its popularity.

Both the cheapness and the availability of Porter had been noted earlier by a Frenchman, Cesar de Saussure, who wrote from London in 1726: 'would you believe it, although water is to be had in abundance in London and of fairly good quality, absolutely none is drunk? The lower classes, even the paupers, do not know what it is to quench their thirst with water. In this country nothing but beer is drunk and it is made in several qualities. Small beer is what everyone drinks when thirsty; it is used even in the best houses and costs only a penny a pot.' [Small beer was a weak ale made by mashing the grain for a second time after a stronger ale had been made.]

'Another kind of beer is called Porter ... because the greater quantity of this beer is consumed by the working classes. It is a thick and strong beverage, and the effect it produces if drunk in excess is the same as that of wine; this Porter costs threepence the pot. In London there are a number of houses where nothing but this sort of beer is sold. There are again other clear beers called ales, some of these being transparent as fine old wine. The prices of ale differ, some costing one shilling the bottle and others as much as one shilling and sixpence. It is said more grain is consumed in England for making beer than making bread.'

So there is doubt among many contemporary observers about the exact period when Porter became a major beer style in London. It is possible that the Porter observed by de Saussure was at first restricted to one area of London. The confusion between three threads and entire was compounded by the fact that Harwood attempted to reproduce the character of three threads with his new brew, and both styles were similar in taste and colour. The use of large amounts of brown malt and blending with stale Brown Beer meant that the beers would have been dark in colour but they would not have had the jet-black appearance that modern drinkers associate with Stout. The reason was that the technology to make black and roasted malts did not exist in the eighteenth century.

Hops by this time were in universal use in brewing – they had arrived late in England in the fifteenth century from Flanders – but many brewers still continued to use other plants and spices to add bitterness and aroma to their ales. Archives record that Porters were heavily hopped at the rate of three pounds per hogshead, a 54-gallon cask. But as eighteenth-century hops were far lower in the acids and tannins of modern varieties, and bitterness levels could not be measured, it is not possible to estimate the hop character of early entires and Porters. With beers matured for long periods, large amounts of hops were used as much for their ability to ward off bacterial infection as for their bitterness.

The importance of water is often overlooked when discussing styles of beer. It was the soft water in London (pumped from wells and not from the River Thames, which was badly polluted) that aided the production of dark beers such as mild ale, brown ale and Porter. London's hegemony was challenged and finally broken in the nineteenth century when new technology and the hard, flinty water from Burton-on-Trent meant that sparkling pale ales could be brewed on a wider commercial basis than the small amounts previously made by country brewers.

Much time and energy has been devoted to unlocking the mystery of the name Porter. For an inexplicable reason, some writers cannot accept the simplest and most plausible case, that it was named after its devotees, London street-market Porters. 'Experts' have come up with suggestions that, as a London Cockney would say, range from the sublime to the gorblimey. I have seen such unlikely 'theories' as erudite country brewers chalking casks with the Latin word 'portare' – to carry – or that the word was a corruption of export, as Porter was the first beer to be sold abroad.

How much easier it is to go to contemporary sources. De Saussure said the beer was called Porter because it was 'consumed by the working classes' while Obadiah Poundage, who had had a long career in London brewing, noted in 1760 that 'the labouring people, Porters etc, experienced its wholesomeness and they assumed to themselves the use thereof, from whence it was called Porter...' The nickname would have been heard daily as the men who delivered supplies to taverns announced their arrival with the cry 'Porter!'

Whatever the doubts and confusion over its origins, by the middle of the eighteenth century Porter – either blended or entire – was big business in London and its success put paid to publican-brewers and even small 'common' brewers such as Ralph Harwood. Demand outstripped their ability to supply. They were replaced by new entrepreneurs who had the capital to invest in vast new breweries that made use of the technical and scientific advances of the industrial revolution. Cast-iron mash tuns and brewing kettles made of copper, both of which retained heat, replaced old and leaky wooden vessels. Steam engines, mechanical pumps, powered rakes for stirring the mash, hydrometers for measuring the sugars in the wort and thermometers for testing temperature were beyond the means of Harwood and his breed.

By Victorian times only four per cent of beer in London was made by publican-brewers, while the great Porter brewers had created enormous power and wealth for themselves. In 1763, the *Gentleman's Magazine* commented caustically on the pleas of overwork among Porter brewers: 'Pining at the hardships they labour under and rolling away in their coaches and six [horses] to their several villas to drown their grief in burgundy and champagne.'

Samuel Whitbread was the most famous of all the London Porter brewers. Even though his annual production was eventually overtaken by some of his competitors, he is a role model for the age. He was the son of a Bedfordshire farmer who may have been descended from Norman French bakers called Blancpain [Whitebread). When Samuel's mother was widowed, she apprenticed him to a London brewer, John Wightman, for the substantial sum of 300. He studied diligently and in 1742 opened his own small brewery in Old Street, close to Harwood's brewhouse. Whitbread did not brew Porter, which suggests the style had not yet entirely dominated the London drinking scene. He made pale and amber ales but within three years had moved to new and bigger premises in Chiswell Street in the area known as the Barbican.

The brewery produced only Porter and Stout Porter. The vast site was one of the wonders of the age, built on a scale never before seen in Britain. King George III and Queen Charlotte visited it in 1787 to see the 'stupendous' steam engine installed by James Watt. The Porter Tun Room had an unsupported roof span 'of which it is exceeded in its majestic size only by that of Westminster Hall'.

At first Whitbread rented 54 buildings in London to store his beer – Obadiah Poundage records that the London Porter brewers vatted their beers for four to five months, half the time of the country brewers – but from 1760 the beer was matured in enormous underground cisterns, each one containing 4,000 barrels, beneath the brewery. The cisterns were kept cool by internal copper pipes: cold water was pumped through the pipes to keep the maturing beer in good condition during hot weather. Brewing was no longer a seasonal business but went on all year round, a further blow to the waning power of the country brewers. Maturing in bulk speeded up production, allowing Whitbread and his competitors to further reduce costs.

The answer to the riddle of why Whitbread brewed both Porter and entire, as seen in the signs on the pub held in the company archive, lies in what happened when the beer had matured. Some was run into large open cooling trays where it was left to acetify to give it the required lactic taste. This was entire. Blended Porter was a mix of fresh ale with mature ale that was held in large wooden vats for several months. Whitbread opened a new vat house at Chiswell Street in the 1790s and the last of the vats was not demolished until 1918.

Blending continued to be carried out in pubs to meet local tastes. In his 1819 *Cyclopaedia*, A Rees noted that: 'All the London Porter is professed to be entire butt, as indeed it was at first, but the system is now altered and it is very generally compounded of two kinds, or rather the same liquor in two different stages, the due admixture of which is palatable though neither is good alone. One is mild and the other stale Porter; the former is that which has a slightly bitter flavour from having been lately brewed; the latter has been kept longer. This mixture the publican adapts to the palates of his several customers.'

Samuel Whitbread was a founder member of 'the beerage', rich and powerful brewers who had the ear of government, often as the result of generous donations to political party funds. Whitbread became the Member of Parliament for Bedford, bought a fine country estate in Hertfordshire, gave generously to charity and had his portrait painted by Sir Joshua Reynolds. In 1812 his son, Samuel II, was brewing 122,000 barrels of Porter and Stout a year, ten times more than Ralph Harwood had managed.

Whitbread, however, had been overtaken by Barclay Perkins (270,000 barrels), Meux Reid (180,000) and Truman Hanbury (150,000). Brewers were part of the driving force of the new industrial order. Within the space of a century, brewing had ceased to be a cottage industry and had become a major commerce.

Competition between the London brewers was fierce, and absurd promotions were staged to stress the size and superiority of individual companies. When Henry Thrale opened a new Porter vat in his Southwark brewery, one hundred people sat down to dine in it. A dinner in Thrale's Anchor Brewery in 1773 took place inside one of the new brewing coppers and was attended by such luminaries of the day as Sir Joshua Reynolds, Dr Samuel Johnson, Oliver Goldsmith and David Garrick. Meux built a vat measuring 18.5 metres (60 feet) wide x 7 metres (23 feet) high. Two hundred guests dined in it. In 1795 Meux added another vat that held 20,000 barrels of beer. This ridiculous bragging was halted only by a terrible tragedy in 1814 when a Porter vat burst at the Horse Show Brewery in Tottenham Court Road, where the Dominion Theatre now stands. The deluge swept away the brewery walls and surrounding streets and houses. Eight people were killed, according to a newspaper report, by 'drowning, injury, poisoning by the Porter fumes or drunkenness'.

The demand for Porter spread outside London. A Bristol Porter Brewery opened at the end of the 1730s, which suggests that some of the contemporary London accounts underestimated the appeal of the beer style. London and Bristol were both great trading ports. London Porter would have gone by boat to Bristol and local brewers moved quickly to control some of the lucrative trade. In 1788 the brewery was bought by a group of Bristol businessmen led by Philip George, who had made his money from distilling and the manufacture of lead shot: the original founder of the brewery, Isaac Hobhouse, had made his fortune from the slave trade. The renamed Philip George and the Bristol Porter Brewery used the great port to export beer. George knew he could never make the brewery pay if he relied on sales in the city and the West Country, where the roads were in an appalling state. George played a key role in selling Porter in Ireland and developing a taste for the beer there. He told his partners in 1789 that eighty barrels of Porter had been shipped to Cork and the same number to Waterford. A further one hundred barrels had been sent to Liverpool with its large and influential Irish community.

In 1792 George sent a traveller, John Bradley, on an exhausting five-month tour of Ireland to promote his beer. In Cork George persuaded a local businessman to take five hundred barrels of Porter, an important deal in a city that was importing 60,000 barrels of British-brewed Porter a year. In Limerick Bradley reported that 'People here complain of the colour being too deep but approve of the body, which they acknowledge considerably superior to the London, therefore they mix them to make the London better and sell it as London Porter where they can, tho' some will prefer at the Pot Houses the Bristol Porter and ask for it as such, which is a proof of its gaining ground here.'

The London brewers were also keen exporters of Porter and Stout. As well as Ireland, they sent their beer to Europe, the Baltic States, the Caribbean, the Far East and the Americas. In 1796 Thrale's brewery supplied Porter 'that would keep seven years' to the Empress of Russia. Thrales was bought by Barclay Perkins in 1781 and Barclays Imperial Russian Stout was so popular in Russia and the Baltic that a brewery was built in Estonia to help meet demand.

In 1795 the author of The History and Antiquities of the Parish of St Saviour, Southwark, wrote this about the Anchor Brewery's beer: 'The reputation and enjoyment of Porter is by no means confined to England. As a proof of the truth of this assertion, this house exports annually very large quantities; so far extended are its commercial connections that Thrale's entire is well known, as a delicious beverage, from the frozen regions of Russia to the burning sands of Bengal and Sumatra. The Empress of all Russia is indeed so partial to Porter that she has ordered repeatedly very large quantities for her own drinking and that of her court.'

Scottish ale was distinctively different to English varieties, lower in hop rates and brewed with generous amounts of dark malt, which meant that Porter would have an obvious appeal to Scots drinkers. The Anderston Brewery in Glasgow was the first to brew Porter. It hired Nathaniel Chivers who had brewed in London and for Guinness in Dublin. He was paid 300 plus 25 expenses to show Anderston how to brew Porter. He made sure his visit to Scotland was profitable by giving identical information to Anderston's rival, John Struthers of Gallowgate. Robert Meiklejohn of Alloa also employed a London brewer to unravel the mysteries of Porter brewing. The two great brewing dynasties of William Younger and Archibald Campbell Younger merged their businesses to ensure a dominant position in the Porter market. Between 1750 and the end of the eighteenth century, the number of commercial breweries in the United Kingdom of Great Britain and Ireland grew from 996 to 1,382 and the largest and most influential of these made Porter.

The Porters and Stouts which today's drinkers associate with the style were the result of further improvements in brewing science and technology in the early nineteenth century. The hydrometer (or saccharometer, as it was first known) meant brewers could measure the fermentable sugars in their beers before fermentation and they discovered the advantages of using pale malt with its higher sugar levels than wood-cured brown malt. Brewers could lower their costs of production by using less malt, an important consideration for brewers the size of Barclay Perkins and the other large London companies.

In 1728, 3,501,888 quarters of malt brewed 6,433,272 barrels of beer in Britain. A century later 3,592,315 quarters of malt produced 8,240,761 barrels. The lifting of the coal tax and the widespread use of coke turned the kilning of pale malt from a country speciality into big business. But pale malt had to be blended with darker malt to give Porter the colour expected by drinkers. According to Rees in 1819: 'The greatest number of the London brewers have given up the brown malt altogether, using pale and amber malt ... From these they procure a liquor of proper strength and they give it both colour and flavour by the addition of colouring matter made from burnt sugar or by burning the sugar of the concentrated wort.' Burnt sugar is called caramel today and is still widely used. When the price of malt rose steeply between 1799 and 1813 brewers turned to all manner of cheap colouring agents: molasses, Spanish liquorice, muscovado sugar and elderberry juice. Less scrupulous brewers used opium, tobacco and extract of poppies. In 1816 the government banned all 'adulterants', as some brewers were actually poisoning their customers.

The brewers were rescued a year later by Daniel Wheeler and his New or Improved Method of Drying and Preparation of Malt. Wheeler had taken the principle of the iron coffee roasting machine and used it to kiln malt to high temperatures of around 450°F/210°C. The deep brown or black malts had little or no fermentable sugars but were soluble in water and a small amount, Wheeler said, 'will suffice for the purpose of colouring beer or Porter.'

Roasted malt, known then as 'patent malt', transformed the production of Porter and Stout. As a result of roasting, black or chocolate malts have an acrid or bitter taste that give to Porter a hint of the smokiness associated with wood-kilned brown malt and the lactic tang of staling. Whitbread grasped the potential of patent malt in the year it appeared (though the company continued also to use wood-smoked malt until at least the 1850s). Barclay Perkins started to use it in 1820.

French and Jupp's, a company that still specialises in roasted malts, built a patent malt factory next to Whitbread in the Barbican to supply the brewery on a daily basis. Dark malts ushered in the era of modern Porters and Stouts. Until the 1820s, these Porters had been dark brown beers, heavily hopped and then matured for several months. Blended

Porters would have varied enormously in flavour as it was left to publicans to mix fresh and stale beers in their cellars to meet their customers' preferences. The self-styled 'Professor of Brewing', W L Tizard, writing in 1857, said that Porter was 'sometimes blinked [not good], often tasting of empyreum [burning vegetable matter], some black, some musty, some muddy, some barmy.' But the brewers were putting such inconsistencies behind them.

Porter and Stout became a distinctive style, a ruby-black beer, made from a single mash, still well matured and with an intensely bitter character from both high hop rates and patent malt. Ironically, all Porter and Stout became 'entire' as brewers began to buy pubs and control cellar quality, but the term fell out of use. When the writer Alfred Barnard, whose *Noted Breweries of Great Britain and Ireland* gives a brilliant snapshot of the brewing industry at a time of profound change, visited Barclay Perkins in 1888 he was surprised to find artists in the sign-writing department of the Anchor Brewery still using the term intire or entire.

'Being much puzzled as to the meaning of the word ... we were obliged to enquire of our guide, who soon made it plain to us.'

Entire had been introduced in the 1720s in order to supply beer to taverns from one cask to avoid the blending of three threads. More than a century later, just as all Porter and Stout became entire butt, its historic roots were being obliterated.

Other more fundamental changes began to affect Porter and Stout. The technology that had enabled commercial breweries to produce the style on a vast scale now became a fetter to future advance.

The failings of the Duke of Wellington's 1830 Beer Act, which allowed anyone to open a beer house for the sum of two guineas, meant that thousands of bankrupt licensed premises were up for sale. They were snapped up by the brewers and the tied house system of public houses directly owned by producers took root. The brewers were anxious to recover the enormous financial outlay they had made in buying pubs and looked for beers that could be sold quickly and profitably. Porter and Stout, vatted for months, represented capital tied up in breweries. The brewers' quest for fast-selling beers coincided with a shift in public taste. In London, working-class drinkers expressed a preference for sweeter mild brown ale while the new and more expensive India Pale Ales brewed in Burton-on-Trent, Tadcaster and Edinburgh were taken up with enthusiasm by the aspiring middle-class of shopworkers and articled clerks who could drink these sparkling, clear ales in bottled form at home, and avoid mixing with their social 'inferiors' in the public house.

The historian R G Wilson has described pale ale as 'the beer of the railway age'. Mild and pale ales were called 'running beers' as they left the brewery as soon as fermentation and a few days conditioning were over and could be sold in pubs after a brief secondary fermentation in cask in the cellar. Porter vats were ripped out of breweries to make way for shallow conditioning vessels for running beers. Whitbread moved swiftly and decisively into pale ale production at the turn of the nineteenth century, and set up bottling depots throughout south-east England to deliver pale ale to middle-class homes.

Porter and Stout, however, remained a major element in a changing beer scene. But the style was dealt a blow by the British government in the First World War from which it never recovered. Driven on by the teetotal Home Secretary David Lloyd George, who thundered that drink was doing more damage to the war effort than German submarines, the government reduced drastically the strength of beer to ensure there were sufficient stocks of barley for bread making. It also restricted malting in order that munitions factories had a plentiful supply of heat and power.

The production of dark malt was badly affected, as it required far more energy to kiln it at the right temperature. Porter and Stout became hard to find and would not have been palatable at greatly reduced strengths.

Towards the end of the war, gravities were forced down to 1030 degrees (gravity roughly translates to modern alcohol by volume by placing a decimal point between the final two figures: for example, 1030 equals 3.0 per cent). The strength was so low that one degree less and such 'near beers' would have been permitted during the Prohibition era in the United States.

Restrictions were more carefully imposed on Ireland. With an increasing demand for Home Rule and the 1916 armed insurrection in Dublin, any attempt to tamper with Irish beer would have been intolerable. Gravities were reduced to a more robust 1042 degrees, and there were fewer restrictions on barley and malt. Irish Porter and Stout flourished and with the near demise of dark beers in Britain it became identified as a style in its own right.

A Pint of Plain

*We sat in Grogan's with our faded overcoats finely disarrayed on easy chairs
in the mullioned snug. I gave a shilling and two pennies to a civil man who
brought us in return two glasses of black Porter, imperial pint measure. I
adjusted the glasses to the front of each of us and reflected on the solemnity of
the occasion. It was my first taste of Porter The Porter was sour to the palate
but viscid, potent. Kelly made a long noise as if releasing air from his interior. I
looked at him from the corner of my eye and said: 'You can't beat a good pint!'
He leaned over and put his face close to me in an earnest manner. 'Do you
know what I am going to tell you,' he said with his wry mouth, 'a pint of plain
is your only man'.*

Flann O'Brien, At Swim-Two-Bird, 1939.

Brewing developed at a slower pace in Ireland than in England.
Ale has a long history in Ireland, dating back some 5,000 years.
St Patrick, the country's patron saint, employed his own brewer,
while St Finnian established the first brewing school on the island.
Monasteries dominated the manufacture and supply of ale for centuries,
a point stressed by the ruins of an abbey still standing within the grounds
of Smithwick's Brewery in Kilkenny.

But Irish ale did not enjoy a good reputation. In the Celtic tradition, it was sweet, heavy and unhopped. Hops struggled to grow and
survive in the damp climate and they were expensive to import as the
English imposed every possible barrier and tariff to impede the growth
of indigenous industries in this outpost of the 'United Kingdom'. When
Arthur Guinness set up as a brewer in the mid-eighteenth century his
ale was made without hops. As in Scotland, distilled liquor, legal and
'moonshine', was the preferred drink of the common people.

In spite of the rapid growth of the population between 1800 and
1845, there was a sharp divide between the English-dominated and
prosperous eastern maritime region based on Belfast, Cork, Dublin and
Waterford, and the rural areas to the west where two-thirds of the population scraped a subsistence living from the land.

There was no market for commercial brewers to exploit in the
countryside. When common brewers did appear they were based in
Cork and Dublin. Both cities were close to the finest barley-grow-
ing regions, and brewers could import equipment and ingredients
through the ports. For a time in the early eighteenth century Beamish
& Crawford of Cork, with an annual production of around 100,000

barrels, surpassed Guinness in size (Guinness was brewing some 66,000 barrels) and together they were the two biggest commercial brewers in the United Kingdom. Most of their sales were of Porter to the burgeoning working class of eastern Ireland.

But the recession that followed the end of the Napoleonic Wars and the terrible famine of 1845-9 devastated the Irish economy and led to a mass exodus of people. Both Beamish & Crawford and Guinness lost almost half their trade. Beamish never recovered its dominant position. Guinness was able to prosper by skilfully building its sales in Ireland through the use of the canal system and, later, the network of railways, and also by adopting a vigorous export policy to Britain.

The records are sketchy but it's thought that Richard Guinness, who was born in the 1690s, was the land agent to the rector of Celbridge in County Kildare. He also brewed ale for the good rector's household. The rector left 100 in his will to Richard's son, Arthur, who bought a small brewery in neighbouring Leixlip (a Viking word meaning 'salmon leap') in 1756.

Like Sam Whitbread, Guinness quickly moved on. Three years later he was in Dublin where he took a 9,000 year lease on a disused brewery in St James's Gate at an annual rent of 45. He agreed to such a long lease as the water on the site came free. Guinness was outraged when the city council later forced him to pay 10 a year for water. The brewery had been up for sale for ten years and was in a bad state of repair. 'The underback is quite decayed,' Guinness complained and noted that only rusted remains of the coppers survived. As a safeguard against failure, he also bought a neighbouring flour mill to provide him both with raw materials and a second business.

By 1787 Guinness was brewing Porter as well as ale. In 1799 he took the momentous decision to phase out ale and concentrate on Porter. Beamish & Crawford had started to brew Porter in 1792. Both breweries did so in an attempt to stem the flood of London and Bristol Porter pouring in through the ports of Cork and Dublin, and to gain a share of this lucrative market. It is not recorded whether Arthur Guinness went to London to study Porter brewing but he did employ a London brewer who had moved to Dublin to offer his skills to the highest bidder.

This was the energetic Nathaniel Chivers who also profited from his foray to Glasgow to teach the Scots how to brew Porter. Guinness's business expanded rapidly. He became the official supplier of Porter to Dublin Castle, the seat of British power, and Master of the Brewers' Guild. He lobbied successfully to get the taxes on beer lowered in order to combat the miseries of gin drinking and to give Irish brewers some leverage over British imports.

As Dublin was the focal point of the Irish canal system, he sent his Porter by barges to all parts of the country. He was the first and only national brewer in Ireland. He opened up the rural market by setting up an adroit system of agents and local bottling stores. Casks of immature Porter would be packed on to barges and would reach maturity during the voyage, ready to be drunk either on draught or run into bottles.

But the main success came from sales of Porter in Dublin and the surrounding areas. Stronger 'Stout Porter', also called Double Stout, was reserved for the export market in Britain, though ordinary Porter, known as 'plain', was supplied to the Irish community in Liverpool. Plain Porter was branded with a single X on casks while Stout Porter was marked XX.

When Arthur Guinness died in 1803 he was worth £10,000. His son, also named Arthur, became Governor of the Bank of Ireland, but devoted a great deal of time to the family business. It was Arthur II who experimented with the recipe of his Porters in such a way as to create the distinctive style that became known as 'Dry Irish Stout'.

Guinness altered the composition of his beers to avoid paying too much tax to the British government. Until Gladstone's budget of 1880, tax was imposed on raw materials. Malt was heavily taxed and made beer expensive to make. Guinness decided to use some unmalted and therefore untaxed roasted barley in his Porters to lower his duty bill. The acrid flavour of the charred barley added bitterness and an unmistakably dry character that marked it out from its English and Scottish rivals. Arthur II also developed the recipe for a special Porter for the export trade that was known as Foreign Extra Porter Stout. Learning from the success of the Burton brewers with their India Pale Ales, Guinness brewed a strong and heavily hopped Porter that would arrive in perfect drinking condition after long and arduous sea journeys to the British colonies.

Guinness and the other Irish brewers were forced to expand outside their country as a result of the devastation caused by the famine and a powerful temperance movement led by a cleric, Father Mathew. Guinness became a cult drink in Britain. By 1840, 82 per cent of Guinness's production was of Stout, mainly for sale in Britain. As the term Porter fell into disuse, Guinness Double Stout, with an original gravity of 1079 degrees, was seen as a quite distinct type of beer to the London-brewed Porters. An illustration in Charles Dickens' *Pickwick Papers* shows a display card advertising 'Guiness Stout'. It was not the first or last time the company name was misspelt. Guinness says ruefully that it has a name half the world can't spell and the other half can't pronounce. At a time when the consistency of beer was variable, Guinness built its reputation on quality and reliability. It also priced Double Stout mid-way between those of London Porter and Burton pale ale, which led to complaints from the English brewers about the tax-dodging activities of their Irish competitors.

In spite of the successful bridgehead built in Britain, the importance of the Irish trade to Guinness cannot be ignored. The company led an assault on the domestic market. It was denied entry into Cork by the presence of Beamish and later Murphy, but started to dominate the rest of the country. As the economy recovered from the ravages of the famine, Porter drinking took off in rural areas and Guinness was often the only brand available. Its success in the Dublin region was so phenomenal that its rivals, including the sizeable Manders, were forced out of business. Between 1855 and 1880 sales of Porter grew sixteen-fold. The year 1885 was the launching pad for Guinness. In the following 21 years output increased from 116,425 to 778,597 barrels. By 1864, it produced more beer than the rest of Dublin's brewers put together. The company accounted for half of Ireland's beer exports and controlled three-quarters of the Irish market outside Dublin. The Guinness brewery had to be completely rebuilt to meet local and international demand in the 1870s. By the end of the nineteenth century Guinness was by far the biggest brewery in Europe. By the end of World War One it achieved the astonishing feat, in a country of just five million people, of becoming the biggest brewery in the world.

Its fortunes had been boosted by the British government's restrictions on strength and malting during the war, restrictions that were far less draconian in a rebellious Ireland. After 1918 Porter and Stout became virtually synonymous with the name of Guinness.

British brewers struggled to rebuild the Stout market and abandoned Porter. In the 1930s Guinness boosted its position in the British market by building a brewery at Park Royal, in London. There were political, as well as economic, reasons for this move. When Eamon de Valera's Fianna Fail party came to power in Ireland in 1932, it refused to pay compensation to former Anglo-Irish landowners. The British government responded by placing higher tariffs on Irish goods. To avoid the price of export Stout rising steeply in Britain, Guinness decided to build a brewery there to supply the local market.

Its amazing success in Britain was aided by the brilliant advertising campaign run by the S H Benson agency, one of whose copywriters was Dorothy L Sayers, better known as a crime writer, the creator of Lord Peter Wimsey. Benson's used the slogans 'Guinness is Good For You' and 'Guinness Gives You Strength' to great effect, with a series of posters showing men carrying giant girders and performing other such incredible feats. Invalids and nursing mothers were advised by doctors to drink a glass of Guinness a day because of its purity and its alleged calorific value.

These days, any suggestion that drinking beer is beneficial to your health is frowned upon by health experts and the goodness of Guinness is no longer featured in advertisements in Britain and the United States. In post-Prohibition America, Guinness was forced to adapt its slogans to 'My Goodness, My Guinness', which was also later used in advertisements in Britain. In 1947 Guinness built a brewery on Long Island to supply the American market but closed it just seven years later. Irish-

Americans, who number forty million, wanted the real McCoy brewed in the old country. It is a rare example of failure by Guinness, yet sales of imported Stout are now flourishing in the United States.

There are more than nineteen versions of Guinness Stout brewed world-wide today and Foreign Extra Stout ('Porter' in the title was dropped long ago and the last draught Porter, brewed for the Belfast area, stopped in the 1970s) is sold in fifty-five countries and brewed under licence in forty-four.

Ten million pints of Guinness are drunk every day throughout the world. It is a cult beer in Africa where the suppliers are not against broadcasting the advantages of Stout, which is regarded as an aphrodisiac. 'There's a baby in every bottle,' they say, though the idea is frowned on by Guinness.

With the massive growth in popularity of lager in the twentieth century, Guinness has been overtaken by other brewing giants, especially those in the United States. Despite this, Guinness remains a major force in brewing, particularly in the Stout market.

STOUT FROM THE MOUNTAIN

Something far more unpleasant than a baby in the bottle encouraged Thomas R Caffrey in Belfast to declare that his Porter and Stout were the purest in the world when he opened his Mountain Brewery in 1897. There had been an outcry in England about arsenic and other poisonous materials used in Porter and Stout and Caffrey, who had taken over a brewery owned by the remarkably named Clotworthy Dobbin, built his reputation on the purity of his beers. Caffrey announced to the public that 'Owing to the seriousness of reports of Beer adulteration by ARSENIC in England, Thomas R. Caffrey, in fairness to his Customers and the General Public, has thrown his Brewery open to the EMINENT PUBLIC ANALYST OF BELFAST. After a most exhaustive examination of the Premises by DR HYDE [sic], who took Samples of all Materials used and also Samples of the Ales, Beer, and Porter from casks selected by him, THOMAS R. CAFFREY has pleasure in submitting the following Report...' There followed a letter signed by Robert Barklie, the Belfast City Analyst, to the effect that 'I have carefully examined all your Brewing Materials, and also the Ales, Beer, and Porters manufactured by you, and taken personally at your Brewery by my Assistant, E. Hyde, BSc, PhD. They are all perfectly free from Arsenic, or other injurious substances.'

Caffrey brewed a Special Draught Porter, Choice Stout, and Extra Double Stout. The purity of his beers inspired the following verse by T. Rafferty of Raglan Street, Belfast:

O, hail to the Mountain that giveth
The PORTER so rich and so pure,
That the Nobles and Lords might partake of
As well as the humble and poor!
The French folk may boast of their Brandies,
The Hollanders talk of their Gin,
But give me the STOUT from the Mountain,
And then I'll feel happy within.

After some swipes at the inadequacy of beers brewed from the waters of the Liffey and the Lee in Dublin and Cork, Rafferty concluded:

Good speed to the NEW MOUNTAIN BREWERY,
May its orders be many and great,
For its PORTER'S the height of perfection;
The Doctors pronounce it first-rate!
Then stop drinking inferior liquors,
And CAFFREY'S
PURE PORTER begin --
And I'm sure you will always be healthy,
For you'll always feel happy within.

Belfast, despite its size and domination of the north of Ireland, was never a major brewing centre and had just three breweries in 1900. Caffrey's remained in the family until the 1950s when it was bought by the local Licensed Victuallers, who eventually sold it on to Bass, the British brewing giant. Porter was brewed until the 1940s. The records do not say when Stout production was stopped but clearly Caffrey's could not compete with Guinness. The Belfast Brewery now produces just keg ales, including a 'Thomas Caffrey's Ale', the first major nitro-keg ale served by a mix of nitrogen and carbon dioxide.

DEAR MURPHY, DEAR BEAMISH

The two Cork-based breweries have had longer and even more dramatic histories than Caffrey's of Belfast. Beamish & Crawford in Cork is the oldest surviving commercial brewery in Ireland. It is based today in a modern brewhouse and offices called the Counting House with a mock-Tudor facade. The offices date from the 1920s. William Beamish and William Crawford, with two other partners, rented premises on the site in 1792 from Edward Allen, whose father Aylmer had started brewing in 1715. Ale had been made here for at least one hundred years.

Beamish and Crawford first called their company the Cork Porter Brewery and their aim was a simple one: to corner a share of the vast Porter market in Ireland's second city. In the year they started in business 60,000 barrels of Porter from England came into Cork. Beamish and Crawford were prosperous businessmen from the north of Ireland and were possibly of Scottish descent. They came south to sell butter and beef but soon saw the potential of Porter brewing. By 1805 they were brewing 100,000 barrels of Porter a year, which accounted for two-thirds of the production of the nine existing Cork breweries. Although sales were hit by recession and the famine, Beamish & Crawford recovered to rebuild the brewery in 1865 at a cost of over £100,000. While it concentrated on X Porter for domestic consumption, a XX Stout Porter was exported to Britain and the United States. Supplies of the latter were on the maiden voyage of the SS Sirius, the first steamship to cross the Atlantic.

Although religious differences are less important today, Beamish & Crawford was known for many years as 'the Protestant brewery'. From the middle of the eighteenth century its main competitor was 'the Catholic brewery' run by the Murphy brothers, James, Francis, William and Jerome. 1854 was not a propitious year to open a new brewery, with the country slowly recovering from years of famine. Cork was well-served with breweries but the Murphy brothers were members of a powerful family that had made most of its fortune from distilling. It had a large stake in Cork Distillers (now Irish Distillers) and the Murphy signature on the label of a bottle of Paddy Whiskey is one of the Cork Murphys. The Murphys may also have decided to go into brewing to challenge the dominance of the Protestant Beamish & Crawford company. The rival families did not socialise, occasional letters were formally addressed 'Dear Beamish' and 'Dear Murphy', and employees were discouraged from fraternising. Curiously, it was the Murphys, not the Beamishes or the Crawfords, who were keen to win knighthoods from the English and were disappointed when no 'gongs' came their way. (The Guinnesses fared better and became the Earls of Iveagh.)

Murphy's brewery was built on premises bought from the former Cork Foundling Hospital. The new company was named Lady's Well

Brewery as a holy well was on the site but water from the well was never used for beer production. A nineteenth-century account of the early years of Cork's newest brewery said:

'Yet, undeterred by all the obstacles that beset their path, undaunted by the influences against which they had to combat, the Messrs Murphy put their shoulders to the wheel and soon came to be recognised as one of the principal brewing establishments in our city'.

Murphy's concentrated on X Porter for the home market and XX Stout for export. The company had agents in several British cities and also fiercely entered the American market. A contemporary source said:

'In America, those of our exiled kith and kin in that country will be in a position to sip of the creamy Stout brewed within sight and sound of some of the most historic scenes of their boyhood's years.'

In 1892, Murphy signed up the circus strongman Sando to endorse its Stout. Eugene Sando or Sandow was a Hungarian and he appeared on Murphy's labels holding a horse off the ground: clearly Guinness was not the only Stout to give you strength.

In 1901 Murphy's took over the substantial Cork brewery of Sir John Arnott and also doubled the size of its tied estate to nearly 200 pubs. In the same year Beamish bought another large Cork brewery, Lane's, and had a tied estate of similar size to Murphy's. Brewery-owned public houses are rare in Ireland and it was the tied estates of the two principal Cork breweries that acted as barricades to the all-conquering giant in Dublin. In 1914 there were 22 breweries in Ireland. In the Irish Republic in 1996 there were seven, of which five – Cherry's, Guinness, Harp, McArdle Moore, and Smithwick's – were part of the Guinness group. Beamish and Murphy were saved from takeover by the size of their tied estates, which made them expensive to acquire.

Guinness finally got a toehold in Cork in the 1920s. A bitter six-week strike by brewery workers closed Beamish and Murphy. The companies were forced to allow their pub tenants to buy beer from other sources and Guinness was the alternative. Today Guinness accounts for half the beer sold in Cork, with the remaining half split between the local brewing companies.

Sean O'Leary and Pat Early are former head brewers at Beamish and Murphy. Now in their seventies and able to socialise – fraternisation was frowned on during their working lives – they give a fascinating insight into Porter and Stout brewing from the mid-1930s. O'Leary joined Beamish in January 1935 as a laboratory assistant at the age of 14. Early went to work for Murphy in 1948 at the age of 21 but he had already worked as a chemist since leaving school. Both of these breweries today have high-tech, computer-controlled plants that can switch from ale to Stout and to lager. But in the 1930s and 1940s they were dedicated Porter and Stout breweries: ale had been phased out when the British withdrew their troops from the Irish Free State in the 1920s.

'We had three beers,' Sean O'Leary said. X was 1035 degrees gravity – that was our Porter but it was called Double Stout in the Dublin area. XXX was 1048 degrees and Export was 1073 degrees.'

Pat Early recalled Porter being brewed for rural workers at harvest time and O'Leary said it was sent in wooden nine-gallon casks called firkins to the countryside when the barley was being gathered in. But Porter never recovered from the lowering of gravities during World War Two. Beamish XXX was reduced to 1042 degrees and that became the standard strength.

The brewhouse at Beamish, where O'Leary rose through the ranks to become head brewer, had five mash tuns and five kettles. After mashing and boiling, the hopped wort was cooled and pumped to open, copper-lined fermenting vessels and mixed with yeast. After 48 hours the fermenting liquid was dropped by gravity into a second bank of fermenters on the floor below.

Much of the detritus known as trub – dead yeast cells, spent hops and other material – was left behind and a cleaner fermentation ensued. The beers were made from pale and dark malts and around nine per cent roasted barley. Brewing sugars were never used. Hops were mainly English Fuggles with some American and European varieties. XX and XXX were hopped at the rate of three pounds per barrel, Export had four pounds. When barley was rationed in the war, oats were used in small amounts to supplement malt.

When the Beamish beers had finished primary fermentation they were racked into hogsheads (54 gallons) and butts (108 gallons) where a second fermentation took place. Additional hops for aroma were added to the casks after three weeks. Sean O'Leary recalled the brewery did little bottling, most of which was carried out by publicans in their cellars. 'Bottled Stout was quite different to cask,' he added. 'It was never bottled until it was nine months old.' It settled down like wine in its casks and was attacked by Brettanomyces [wild] yeasts. The beer was sharp and lactic. Some fifty years after British brewers had abandoned the vatting of beers for long periods, the Irish were still using the methods of the eighteenth century Porter pioneers.

Pat Early mashed only once a week at Murphy due to the enormous size of the mash tun, which produced sufficient wort to make one thousand barrels of beer. In common with Guinness, the mash tun was called a 'kieve' from the old French word cuivre, meaning a copper vessel. Hops and wort were boiled in coal-fired coppers.

Until the 1960s Irish Stouts were served by a system known as the 'high cask and low cask'. Drinkers demanded a good, creamy head on their beer. This was achieved by racking some finished Stout into casks, leaving it for twenty-four hours and then blending it with unfermented wort and yeast. The casks were then stored for ten days while the wort and yeast started a third fermentation. In pubs the casks were placed on stillages with the highly-conditioned Stouts on the top level and casks with less lively beer below.

'The top casks were known as the gyle casks,' Sean O'Leary recalled. (Gyle is a brewers' expression for a finished batch of beer.) 'The publicans would fill glasses three-quarters full from the high cask and then top them up with flat beer from the low cask.' The gyle casks had timbers one and a half inches thick to withstand the pressure of the fermenting Stout.

The days of cask-conditioned Stout came to an end in the 1950s and 1960s. In Britain, where brewers directly own many pubs, they can control cellar quality and train publicans to look after cask-conditioned ales and Stouts. It is a far more difficult task in Ireland where most of the bars are free from brewery ownership. Sean O'Leary and Pat Early said that Guinness was experimenting with filtered and artificially pressurised Stout as early as the 1940s. In the 1950s the group introduced a pressurised Stout served from a horizontal metal container that was nicknamed 'the iron lung'. The vessel had separate compartments for filtered Stout, carbon dioxide and nitrogen. When the tap was opened, the gasses propelled the beer to the bar and caused a fascinating and eddying swirl in the glass, which slowly and temptingly separated into black body and creamy head. Although the iron lung was replaced by a conventional upright keg, Guinness had overnight refashioned the Irish Stout market. Appearance became almost as important as quality and taste. A dense collar of creamy foam on top of a glass of Stout became obligatory. I remember queuing to get into a pub in London's Fleet Street when Draught Guinness was launched in London in the 1960s and impatiently salivating as the beer slowly ran into the glass and then magically separated into liquid and head. Pouring the perfect pint became part of the folklore of Irish Stout. A Guinness advertising campaign showed a pint with a smiling face drawn in the foam: there might not be a baby in every bottle, but there was pleasure in every pint.

In a still largely rural and conservative country, many Irish drinkers hankered after the old methods of serving cask-conditioned Stout. But Beamish and Murphy, reluctantly at first, were forced to follow in Guinness's footsteps. As minority brewers in even their native city, they would have lost even more market share to the Dublin giant if they had not gone down the pressurised route. They had been selling their tied pubs and in the 1960s both companies faced financial crises. Beamish at one stage was confronted with the ignominy of being taken over by Guinness and was saved when the company was bought by Canadian Breweries. The Canadian group, later renamed Carling O'Keefe, swept into Cork with a mission to convert the Irish to the pleasures of Carling Black Label lager. It had no knowledge of Stout and the deep and almost mystical roots the beer style has in Ireland. Carling made only limited inroads into the Stout market but Beamish's brands suffered from being sidelined as lager was zealously promoted. When Carling O'Keefe was bought by Foster's, Beamish found itself briefly owned by an Australian company. Foster's also controlled the large British brewing group, Courage, which gave Beamish a much-needed entr into the British pub market. A further twist was given to this convoluted history when Courage merged with the Scottish and Newcastle group in 1995. Beamish now supplies Britain's second biggest brewing conglomerate, Scottish Courage.

Murphy had an even more turbulent time. In the 1960s it went into partnership with the English Watney Mann group to brew Watney's Red Barrel keg ale under licence. At the time keg ale was revolutionising the British beer scene and Watney Mann, with post-colonial arrogance, thought the Irish would swallow Red Barrel as enthusiastically as the English. For its part, Murphy assumed the Irish would accept the English ale almost as an indigenous brew, as there is a tradition of brewing copper-coloured ales in Ireland. Red Barrel flopped in Ireland. Even worse, Murphy's Stout, marketed by both Watney Mann and Bass Charrington in Britain as Colonel Murphy's Stout, was the victim of double dealing. According to the magazine Business and Finance in 1970, the Stout gained a 'high level of acceptance' but 'the investment and effort required to catch up with the public awareness of Draught Guinness would have been less profitable to the group [Watney Mann] than the sale of a product already successfully marketed'.

Both Watney Mann and Bass Charrington abandoned Murphy in favour of Guinness, plunging the Cork company into deep crisis. It went into receivership and was bought by a consortium of Cork publicans with financial assistance from the government: the Taoiseach at the time was Jack Lynch, a Cork man who was determined to help a local company and prevent even greater brewing power residing in Dublin. Eventually Murphy was bought by the Dutch group Heineken. This gave Murphy's Irish Stout, as it is badged today, massive support in international markets. In particular, Heineken's links with Whitbread gave Murphy an important opening in Britain, the largest market in the world for Stout. It is a growing market, still dominated by Guinness, which today brews more versions of Stout at its London brewery than at any time since Park Royal opened in the 1930s. But the two Cork Stouts are building steady sales in Britain and Beamish makes much of the fact that it is the only Irish Stout sold in Britain that is actually brewed in Ireland. Most of the Murphy's Stout sold by Whitbread is brewed at its Magor plant in Wales. An Irish Stout brewed in Wales? It sounds like an Irish joke.

Murphy enjoys considerable success in the United States. Beamish was stopped from having similar success in the 1980s when the owners of Jim Beam whiskey took legal action to stop the Stout being sold in the US on the grounds of product confusion. (Readers will be immediately struck by the similarity of a glass of bourbon whiskey to a pint of Irish Stout.) Eventually Beamish won the case but the court costs involved were a tremendous drain on the company's financial resources and it now has to work hard to catch its rivals.

In spite of these vicissitudes, Irish Stout is a major force on the world brewing scene. It has bucked the trend towards pale beers, lager in particular, and it is a potent symbol of Ireland's struggle for nationhood and for independence.

Brewing Section

ACKNOWLEDGEMENTS

This is the second Homebrew Classics book for CAMRA. Once again I feel I am only the deliverer. Much of the strategic work, which has made this book possible, has gone on behind the scenes over years. Our thanks go to the Durden Park Beer Circle, for all their work in sorting out brewing methods and recipes from old brewing registers. This is such a mammoth task, that had I had to do it, this book would never have been written. Furthermore, we must all be grateful for their selfless attitude to their own labours. Who else would simply say, "use it, copy it, it's in the public domain!"

James Mc Crorie of Durden Park Beer Circle has always been a sounding board off which I can bounce ideas. Not only did he reply with sound criticism, but he also ferrets out the bits of information, which so often elude us writers, and in the spirit of Durden Park, he has made the huge amounts of material available for my use. He, Bill Cooper and Colin Penrose have critically evaluated the text. They are not happy with it, but that is healthy. I have had to draw a line under the task, but they can improve on the research when their time and energy allows.

The British Library staff, were as usual, brilliant. They are the most helpful and knowledgeable body to whom we writers can turn.

The Brewing Archive of Glasgow University reviewed *Homebrew Classics IPA*, and approved. So we have kept the same format – Craft Brewing on Historical Principles.

Thanks to you all.

Clive La Pensée   Whitby June 7, 2002

Introduction

The second of the series of Homebrew Classics for CAMRA books was always going to be a nightmare. Porter and Stout. Help!

Ask ten brewers and you'll get eleven opinions, is the brewer's maxim and it can never be more true than for Brown Beers. They have their origins in the 17th century. I've tried to make clear how different the approach to scientific discovery was before the industrial revolution. We take rational thought for granted. How else can we know a plane will fly before it has left the drawing-board, or maintain the manic pace of change of the 20th century into the 21st. It is so hard for us to comprehend the minds of men and women three hundred years ago, who never thought rationally, at least in our sense of the word, and yet have made so many things work, so elegantly and with such precision. Furthermore, because they only base their knowledge on what they have already experienced, their method of recording that experience is so different to ours.

I told CAMRA that it would be a long hard road, and I'd rather make two books of it, brown beers and Porter, but they wanted the Porter Stout symbiosis and for obvious reasons.

I've been told I failed to inject enough humour into this subject. I answered, "you read 18th century texts for a year of your life and try not to let it rub off on you!" There is no humour to be found! Life was serious and a daily fight for existence.

I've been told that this one is not a page-turner. True. I hope it is an historical contribution and I've tried to put Stout and Porter into their historical context. How can we understand the beer if we ignore the people and their reason for brewing it? There are plenty of excellent homebrew books on the market with pages of recipes. I hope this book adds value to their contribution.

Although co-writers of this book Roger Protz and I have chosen different approaches. There's more than one way to skin a rabbit and he took the other way. I look forward to the dialogue and battles Roger and I will have in the future. They will demonstrate how alive and well Real Ales and Craft Brewing really are. Organisations such as Durden Park, CAMRA and the Craft Brewer's Association are custodians of our past. I believe we must understand where we have come from before we can shape the future properly. Hence my respect for them and my contribution to putting Porter into context.

Stout and Porter Brewing

by Clive La Pensée.

Copyright Clive La Pensée September 2001.

"Whether London Porter is entitled to the praises bestowed on it by its admirers, is not for us to determine; its nutritious qualities have been much vaunted, and doubtless have been, and still are, much overrated. Its chief distinction lies in its peculiarly agreeable flavour, aided by its flushing, mantling effervescence: these characteristic qualities are produced by hops of a peculiar quality, and malts prepared and dried by a peculiar process, assisted by a peculiar method of conducting the fermentation."

The Brewer 1863.

1700 – 1760

1.1 PORTER, THEOLOGY AND
THAT BASTARD JONES

What sort of country was England during the eighteenth century? What sort of beverage was Porter, that it became the most important item on any meal table? Where did it part company from Stout beers, which had been around for many years? Why was it rarely mentioned in good company? How was it brewed, why was it brewed and why did it disappear into relative obscurity so rapidly? Did it ever really exist or was it merely a cunning piece of marketing for other (Stout) brown beers, which were already available?

Not a bad list to start with and if I've answered all those questions and provided some recipes for Porter and its brown beer precursors and successors such as Stout by the time we go to print I will be well pleased.

To the first question. What sort of country was England during Porter's emergence as the drink of the working man and gentry?

To discover more about England in the 18th century I turned to Fielding, novelist, lawyer and fierce social critic of the time. His most famous work is *Tom Jones,* which has been the subject of two highly successful films since 1960.

Tom was a bastard, taken in by a man without issue of his own. Squire Allworthy was soundly criticised for this act of charity for it was generally believed that not only should the erring parents be soundly punished, but any leniency toward the child would also encourage such profligate behaviour in others. Allworthy was sensible to this accusation and, as the local magistrate, felt that he could not leave young Tom too much freedom. He engaged as Tom's two teachers Mr. Thwackum, a theologian and Mr. Square whose main strength was pondering the ethics of every situation. The presence of Square was just as well for Thwackum was a brute, who would have flogged Tom at any occasion. Fortunately for Tom he was only beaten when Square failed to convince Allworthy and Thwackum that Tom's actions did indeed have some ethical value. Thwackum and Square were joke characters as was Tom's stepbrother, the odious Master Blifil. He provided for sibling rivalry by aligning himself to Thwackum and doing his best to undo Tom at every opportunity during their hours together with their two teachers. They were of course, also rivals in love, although Blifil never really stood a chance against the heroic Tom.

Henry Fielding gives us insight enough into the arguments, which occupied our pedagogues each time Tom transgressed. These discussions often took place over dinner, at which Claret was invariably served. There was no mention of Porter, although it was the stable drink of the time. In the film versions much is made of Tom's good looks and ability to get laid at the mere sight of a pretty pair of legs. His conquests often took place in public houses, and on one occasion were preceded by huge quantities of oysters and beer. We may assume it was Porter for these two complement each other well. Stout brewed with oyster extract is still available on supermarket shelves today.

In such arguments Thwackum quoted the scriptures and Square the Greek Philosophers. Squire Allworthy had to pass judgement. Where was the scientist? He hadn't been invented or more accurately he was called a "natural philosopher" and he wasn't always a he. Where was the mathematician? Encompassed in Greek Philosophy, which is why Fielding treats Square with greater sympathy than poor Thwackum ever receives. There was never a suggestion that anything not encompassed in theology or philosophy would be needed in order to lead a good and wholesome 18th century life.

Of course Fielding was very critical of the theology/philosophy corner and spent much of his own life working to alleviate the results of crime and deprivation in the eighteenth century. The picaresque novels he wrote were preceded by those of Daniel Defoe, which had a similar plea, but literature was not the tool with which to rationalise society. Maybe beer was!

We are not to believe that science played no part in eighteenth century life. Isaac Newton died in 1727, before Porter brewing was at its height, but he ignored the established university curriculum and applied himself to mathematics and natural philosophy, which we would now call science. This new discipline was to wait many years to find its way into practical applications such as brewing, and then only in the cities where new ideas and technology were rapidly embraced. Of course the new technologies were exported from the cities to the countryside as evidenced by the agricultural revolution and enclosures, but do not seem to have impacted on brewing practices very much.

The ideas and scientific principles used may not be recognised as such by us nowadays. Science in the eighteenth century relied on *empiricism*, which was very much the order of the day. This was the philosophical doctrine that affirms that all knowledge is based on experience, while denying the possibility of spontaneous ideas or *a priori* thought. Until the 20th century the term *empiricism* was applied to the view held chiefly by the English philosophers of the 17th, 18th, and 19th centuries. Brewers had centuries of experience and so considered themselves to have "the knowledge" and were not easily deflected from this belief. Brewers were the great empiricists in everyday life. They still remain the great pragmatists. Hence beer strength was not only measured in darkness and texture because that seemed an obvious yardstick, but also because pale malt was difficult to make and hard to keep. The malt was fired using wood, which was available. This may have been dry faggot and often resulted in excessive heating, due to poor temperature control. Low diastatic power and a caramelised outer coating to the grain resulted. Such malt was eminently suitable for brown beer brewing.

Let us assume that pale malt was made in any quantity. Malt is hygroscopic and takes water from the air. It is then said to be "slack" and is quite useless for brewing, unless it is reheated to dry it. This still left it without diastatic power but dry enough to be crushed without going pasty and prevented wastage. I assume a genuinely pale beer was difficult to come by unless one had the price. There were always economic as well as philosophical reasons for brewing dark.

So if the eighteenth century saw the birth of the industrial revolution, why was Allworthy still happy to base all decision on theological and philosophical premises? This may have had much to do with the population distribution in England at the time. At the beginning of the century most centres of population were on the coast, but the growth of the industrial town was the single biggest change during the age of Porter. Allworthy ran agriculture in his local area and was concerned with rationalising the means of production in that sphere of activity. He didn't need the steam engine for land enclosures and had Fielding written a sequel, I don't doubt that a Squire Allworthy of the beginning of the nineteenth century would have been indistinguishable in attitudes from the Allworthy who was stepfather to Tom Jones.

We are not told this in the novel, but I have no doubt that Allworthy's cook was responsible for brewing the beer for the estate. Her brew house may have doubled as a washroom on Mondays so she needed to consider the organisational requirements of the housekeeper. Cook probably didn't consider the logistics of selling her beer outside the house. According to Mathias (*History of Brewing 1700-1830)* the few rural breweries that there were delivered only to a seven-mile radius. That was already an awesome task if the weather was anything but perfect for there were no roads as we know them. Even the lowliest farm worker brewed his own beer. This meant that the steam engine, iron bridges and canals had little impact on the rural communities away from the new industrial towns.

By the end of the eighteenth century the canal network had made the transport of beer and grain quite easy. Implements made from iron and then steel were readily available, the steam engine had reached a level of sophistication which made mine pumping a regular business and the resulting increase in coal production meant that steam engines could be more easily employed in all areas of industrial production. More implements could be made from iron and steel, and coke production allowed a clean controlled manufacture of pale malt. Coke was relatively clean as a fuel and rapidly gave rise to town gas, which brought with it volume glass making, glasses as drinking vessels together with the hydrometer and thermometer. Chemistry, Biology and Engineering were born and Pale Ale brewing for domestic or export trade were soon to produce the new discipline we now call Biochemistry.

It is important to remember that in a society with a highly decentralized means of production, new inventions, ideas and knowledge were very slow to have an overall impact. Monckton (*A History of English Ale & Beer*) dates the invention of the mercury in glass thermometer (suitable for brewing) by Fahrenheit as 1714, but its introduction to brewing as 60 years later. Part of the problem is revealed by Richardson, writing in 1784 (*Philosophical Principles of the Science of Brewing*). The thermometer meant a humble servant would have to work with exactitude and this he feared. It was an attack on his empirical knowledge. It also meant that his master had to teach him to read and count or else do the back-breaking work himself. Brewing was indeed turning the world on its head (appendix 2).

The hydrometer (saccharometer) had an even more difficult passage. Invented in the 1760s, Monckton reminds us it took an act of Parliament by Gladstone in 1880 to force its complete use. Here was a classic conflict between industry and state. The maltster and brewer were quite happy to keep the public and the taxman in the dark, but the government wanted its excise collected accurately. Why did it take the government 100 years to realise they were being worked over by the gentry? The government were the gentry and in 2002 we are still (not quite) shot of them.

The hydrometer and thermometer meant a rapid increase in brewing knowledge as meaningful records on individual brews could be kept. Brewers realised what a waste of money dark malt was and drinkers could see what they were drinking and rather liked a clear light brew in a glass container. Many writers on brewing knew the truth about Porter malt as early as 1734, but this doesn't seem to have influenced the majority of brewers and their techniques until 100 years later. Was this was a result of *empiricism* and the fact that theoreticians had a problem delivering the wisdom to brewers, many of whom couldn't read, or was it just plain avarice that caused brown malt to hold sway until it was no longer economically advantageous to the commercial brewer to continue to use it?

And in all this Tom Jones and his sons, as Allworthy's heirs, continued to brew their Brown Beer exactly as it had been a hundred years earlier. They still relied on the local cleric for information and spiritual guidance and were little touched by the rapidly growing town breweries, which, by the middle of the century were brewing huge quantities for the expanding industrial towns. In fact it seems that only the

Porter breweries rose to massive production in the eighteenth century, while country ale brewers were much the same by 1800 as they had been in 1700.

Sambrook (*Country House Brewing in England 1500-1900* 1996) asserts that Porter brewing was not commonplace in the countryside. If the landed gentry developed a taste for the drink when they went up to town they would purchase bottled Porter for their domestic consumption. This is an issue, which we may never be able to be precise about. It is unlikely that all country houses kept records, or that all records are available and none have been destroyed and that Sambrook has had access to all available records. Most importantly, if Porter was nothing but a marketing fad for brown beers already being produced, there was no reason for Alworthy's cook, or any other country brewer, to adopt the new name. Hence there is no reason for Porter to appear in rural brewing records. Ellis (*London & Country Brewer 1734*) doesn't mention Porter and in later editions refers to it as a new name for an existing beer. In the 19th century professional brewers often used the names Porter, Brown Beer and Stout without distinction. Hence Sambrook may have asked the wrong question.

Nevertheless it is surprising that in the country houses she investigated Porter made such little impact, especially as Amsinck in the 1830s still provides a separate recipe for a "Country Porter" (recipe 20).

The extreme difficulty of transporting bottled or casked beer beyond the canal network must have made such purchases risky, but then we know that Allworthy drank Claret so risks were obviously a part of daily life if you wanted a varied diet and refreshment. Sambrook does find the occurrence of inventories containing reference to bottled Porter. This does not in itself indicate it was purchased. Speciality beers were bottled if they were to keep a long time.

The point to all this is that beer production in the eighteenth century was not a homogenous entity, because the country as a whole was anything but homogenous. The country house brewery was as important sociologically as the large breweries in London Town, but totally different in scale, expertise, philosophy and technique. Both ends of this spectrum will need considering in any book on Porter and Stout. What is not clear is how entrenched the ideas of the seventeenth century, (dominated by theology and Greek Philosophy) were in the minds of the city dwellers, most of whom had moved from the countryside to find new jobs in the expanding cities. We do know that during the eighteenth century the balance of population living in the country shifted dramatically in favour of the town. This means that the countryside cannot be ignored even though Porter was essentially a city commodity. The population shift must have meant that the ideas prevalent in the cities were constantly being refreshed with reactionary rural thinking.

So if England wasn't a homogenous country, and scientific investigation wasn't ruled by a single philosophy, there is no reason to suppose that Porter was the same drink to all people. We shall return time and again to the differences in England between the town and the countryside, to the battles fought in the Royal Society between the Newtonian *a priori* mathematicians and astronomers and the *empiricist* botanists and zoologists and finally, as the large breweries increased their hegemony, we shall see how the private brewers, (by 1790 this usually meant the town dweller families) made Porter their drink and in some cases even attempted to make a poor mans' claret from it so that they too could ape the tables of the rich and worthy. We shall see how the name changed from Stout Beer to Brown Beer and Entire Butt, often spelt Intire Butts, to Porter and finally back to Stout and then again Porter.

To summarize, it would appear that Porter at the beginning of the 1720s was a Brown Beer, strong enough to have been called a "Stout Beer" but due to some reason locked in urban myth came to be known as Porter. It was all things to all people and never really formed a style. By the middle of the 19th century it was indistinguishable from Stout, just brewed a bit thinner. We shall have to accept the painful truth that if Porter is not definable with a homogeneous style then neither can a book on Porter and Stout be about a single style of beer. Brewers in the 18th and 19th centuries were often content to talk about "brown beers," when searching for a style, but that doesn't sound fashionable to our 21st century ears. One thing hasn't changed since 1722 – the power of fashion!

1.2 EIGHTEENTH CENTURY PORTER MALT

Porter malt was also known as Brown or Blown malt in the 19th century. Brown malt had been around for several years out of necessity. As indicated, until the mining of sufficient cheap anthracite, (often referred to as Welch Coal, Swansea Coal or Culm), and the later production of coke, brown malt was made using whatever wood was available for drying. This frequently resulted in malt charred on the outside and having taken up the properties of the wood smoke. Different degrees of charring occurred depending on the type of wood, its dryness (e.g. time of year, rainy or drought period etc.) and skill of the maltster. Until the common use of coke for firing there was no such thing as a common Porter malt. Brewers used anything that wasn't pale and it was often fearfully dark. I have already laboured the point that there was never any homogenous Porter, Stout or Brown Beer production. This is especially evident from 18th century sources. Different areas had different firing materials available and so there were unknown hundreds of different brown malts being made and used in England each having the qualities of its firing material. The above argument applied equally to so called "Stout Beers" which were the forerunners of Porter. Does this mean that Porter was never anything other than a speciality Stout?

But firstly a little about malt making.

Since the beginning of brewing some 5000 years ago barley has been the favoured grain. This is because the husk on barley makes it suitable for malting. The reason for turning barley into barley malt is to make the starch within the barley seed available for the brewer to convert into maltose, which is a fermentable sugar. The barley seed stores energy as starch by taking carbon dioxide from the air, water from the ground and using sunlight as an energy source to drive the photosynthesis reaction, which makes starch. Starch is a so-called polysaccharide, which means it has lots of glucose units joined together (poly = many and saccharide = sugar). In nature the seed swells with starch during the summer months when lots of sunlight is available, dries out before the harvest and then becomes dormant due to the lack of water. This dormancy is ended when the seed hits damp warm earth whereupon it takes up water and awakes expecting to form a new barley plant. Starch is present in the seed as an energy store to tide the seed over until it can throw out a leaf and start to photosynthesise and make its own food. Starch is insoluble in water, which is just as well or it would be washed out the seed when it rains. This insolubility means that starch itself cannot nourish the new germinating plant. Only water-soluble material can pass through the membranes and into the powerhouse within the seed. So the first step in a seed germinating is to convert the starch into useable water-soluble sugar and for this the seed has a ready store of enzymes. These are protein molecules exactly the right shape to unlock the massive coiled starch structure and render it as water soluble maltose, a disaccharide. Maltose is not only the sugar which supports the new barley plant with energy but is also a fermentable sugar which the brewer can use to make alcohol and carbon dioxide. It is the maltster's job to call up the enzymes, which the brewer will use to convert the starch to maltose, by emulating the method used in nature. Nature's way has certain disadvantages, the main one being it allows the barley seed to waste valuable corn substance by supporting growth of the new barley plant. The maltster alters the conditions of germination in order to restrict the use of the corn's starch by letting the plant germinate under controlled conditions.

The exact nature of germination of barley in a malting has only been understood for around 100 to 150 years. This tells us that the road from picking barley to making beer, already a process, which predates history, must have been learned by observation and very well those early maltsters and brewers must have observed! The earliest maltsters even knew how to prevent excessive corn substance from being lost by the barley growing and this is done by drying the malt under very controlled conditions, which protect the enzymes and starch. This kills the barleycorn and we give it a new name "malt". Malt also has a better shelf life than barley.

When the brewer wants to make beer he adds water. Although the malt is dead, the water (now called mash liquor) carries the enzymes into the wet starch where they can begin the process of converting the starch to maltose. This step happens during mashing.

Because maltsters knew they had to dry malt to make it keep and give it other qualities such as colour, but they didn't understand the enzyme and starch part of the story, they put up with the drying process being a pretty haphazard affair and if the malt got a bit burned then dark beer was brewed. They didn't realise that dark malt was a waste of time and money in brewing terms.

So the early maltsters (until around 1800) steeped the barley in huge cisterns at around 8°C (48°F) for an average of 72 hours in order to awaken the dormant seed. The process was later enhanced by blowing air through the steep water in order to sweep out the carbon dioxide being produced by the seed as it began to germinate. This saved changing the steep water every few hours.

Once the barley has taken up sufficient water (around 45%) the water is drained off and the barley left to complete germination. This takes another 5 days at around 14°C (58°F) and the heap must be frequently turned to prevent the new roots, which begin to grow rapidly, from matting. It also prevents heat build up, which would lead to hot spots and quick growth in localised parts of the heap, and of course keeps the moisture evenly distributed. Any areas of dryness would lead to slow growth. Excessive wetness causes the barley to be ruined by mould infections. During this time some enzymes are actually produced within the corn and others already present in the dormant barley achieve their more soluble form. In nature these processes are allowed to storm ahead and a new plant is created. But growth occurs at the expense of starch, which in ideal malt should be yielded up to the brewer. Hence growth is limited by the maltsters' handicraft.

He observes the new shoot (acrospire) forming under the husk. The latter protects the acrospire from being damaged during turning. For pale malt 99% of the corns should have a shoot length $^2/_3$ the length of the corn length.

Darker malts are more tolerant of shoots longer than the magic fraction and less sensitive to a poorly turned heap. Furthermore, barley with acrospires, which have been allowed to exceed the length of the corn also allow the enzymes to take on their soluble form. This gives the beta-amylase more time to be formed and so the malt has greater diastatic power. In Germany a variety called *Kraftmalz* has always been available to deal with heavy grain types or poorly grown malts. Such malts produced with greater diastatic activity appeared to produce better starch conversion during the mash. What wasn't always appreciated in the early eighteenth century was the waste of corn substance involved in allowing grains to over modify (i.e. begin to convert starch into sugar for growth). It seemed to brewers who had no hydrometer to allow them to check extract efficiency that a well-grown and over-modified malt was maybe something of a good thing.

The second error in dark malt production came during the drying phase. All malts must be carefully dried down to around 2% water by weight in order to give them any kind of shelf life. They then undergo a roasting to give them the correct degree of colour. Drying at high temperatures while still wet destroys the enzymes and makes starch conversion impossible by simple mashing. In the days when enzymes were treated as a religious spirit and water seen as the supPorter of all life, our *empirical* brewers had no way of appreciating that water is a highly reactive polar molecule well capable of seeing off a sensitive protein chain of the alpha and beta amylase type. And so it was that wet green malt was regularly taken and dried at astounding temperatures. In 1712 maltsters were adjured to take wood that had been dried for at least 5 or 6 years, but this increased expense without really standardising the malt quality. Certainly by 1736 many brewers knew of the folly of dark malt brewing and making dark malt by burning good green malt over a hot fire. Although the hydrometer had not been invented brewers had started to weigh their worts. This was done by comparing the weight of a barrel of water to the weight of a barrel of wort. The extract was then expressed in pounds per barrel more than water. So if the information was available, why keep using high dried malts for another 100 years? Empiricism dies hard when you can't read or write. What use is the 1736 *London & Country Brewer* to an illiterate brewer? Pale malt was so difficult and expensive to make that in *New Method of Drying Malt* by John Allen

(1730) he asked the King to protect his idea for a machine to dry malt without the risk of it taking the taste of smoke or burning.

Essentially water was boiled and the green malt placed on a sheet (6 ft x 20 ft) above the boiling water. Thus the temperature of the drying surface could never exceed 100°C (212°F). 20-25 bushels could be dried at once and a 4-inch layer of green malt took 18 hours to dry or 3 inches was finished in 12 hours. Any firing material could be used.

No temperatures within the body of the drying malt were recorded. In my experience the latent heat of vapourisation would keep the malt well below 100°C (212°F) but this must have still counted as pretty rude treatment compared to modern day techniques.

This method was supposed not to use more fuel, which I find hard to believe but, most interestingly, Allen asserts drinkers of coal dried malt condemned the flavour of straw or wood malt and vice versa. Here was the method of preventing the quality of the firing material altering the nature of the brown malt, in areas where culm was not available. And here we have the rub. Generally our 18th century drinker expected the flavour of his firing material to be imparted to the beer. Under such circumstances Allen's machine was always on a loser and we shall find it difficult to recreate an 18th century Porter. The only help at hand is a *Rauchmalz* stocked by Brupaks. This is still dried over open beech faggots and has the distinctive flavour of the wood. It has its home in the German City of Bamberg where a smoked dark beer is a local speciality. This dark beer called *Schlenkela,* is as close as we shall get to a genuine Porter from the early 18th century.

The power of the Porter Myth must have been enormous. In 1913 Thomas Mann began writing *Der Zauberberg*. After days of travelling from Hamburg to Switzerland the main character Hans Castorp arrives in a sanatorium high in the Alps. He doesn't ask for *Schlenkela*, but enquires of his cousin, "Can one get Porter up here?" In fact he can't and has to settle for a Kulmbacher, which is so strong that it is nearly his undoing. And in Tolstoy's short story *Hadji Murád* which takes place in Chechnyá in 1852, Porter gets a mention as the preferred drink.

The brewer wanted carefully dried malt for economic reasons, but did the drinker? My grandfather still believed pale beers were dark ones with all the goodness taken out. Even assuming the maltster and brewer were enlightened as to the virtues of pale ale brewing they still had to convince the drinker. Public demand was still difficult to shift in a decentralised community with no media to speak of. And of course there is the question of how hard the brewer and maltster tried. Dark beers cover a multitude of brewing sins and there was an economic spin off for the brewer. Hops have always been the most expensive commodity to any brewer. If you make a Porter using only brown malt it will be so black and bitter from the burnt malt that the quality of hop flavour becomes something of an irrelevancy.

The question that also needs answering is how much brown malt went into brown beers like Stout or Porter. Did brewers really make Porter with only high dried, not to say burnt malt during the first half of the 18th century? The evidence is that indeed 100% brown malt Porters were generally brewed. Combrune in his *The Theory and Practice of Brewing (London* 1762) indicates that brown malt was started with only "the very palest of malt." Such malt if carefully dried would have the greatest diastatic power. From his description of dampness it may have even been undried green malt with as much as 40% water. Such a drying method would bring it close to some 19th century blown malts and would have destroyed all enzyme activity within the malt, rendering it useless for providing extract....unless....a good amount of pale or amber malt was added to the grist too. This was certainly the case 100 years later but in 1762 Combrune records:

"In an earthen pan about 2 feet in diameter and 3 inches deep, I put as much of the palest malt, unequally grown, as filled it on a level to the brim. This I placed over a little charcoal lighted in a small stove, and kept continually stirring it from bottom to top.

At first it did not feel so damp as it did half an hour after. In about an hour more it began to look of a bright orange colour on the outside, and appeared more swelled than before. I then masticated some of the grain and found them to be nearly such as are termed brown malts. On stirring and making a heap of them towards the middle, I placed therein at half depth, the bulb of my thermometer and found that it rose to 140 degrees: the malt felt very damp, and had but little smell."

"At 165 degrees I examined in the same manner as before, and could perceive no damp; the malt was very brown and on being chewed some small black specs appeared.

At 180 degrees the water was nearly all evaporated.

At 210 the malt hissed and smoked abundantly. $^2/_3$ the corn were perfectly black, the rest brown."

Unlike the steam malter recorded by Allen, it seems fair to assume that Combrune was actually applying a direct heat to the green malt, hence his description " the malt felt very damp.... The water was nearly all evaporated". His statement "Palest malt, unequally grown," also leads me to believe he was experimenting with green malt, otherwise he could not have known it to be unequally grown (i.e. acropspires of varying length under the husk). Under such circumstances it is unlikely that any diastatic power was left in the malt and subsequent mashing probably resulted in little useful fermentable extract being available. If, as I am speculating, Combrune did start with green malt then his method of making brown malt was the precursor to that described by Stopes 100 years later. Stopes leaves us in no doubt that Brown Malt was made in Hertfordshire by heating green malt very strongly. The steam escaped with such force that it caused the grain to swell and even burst. The smouldering husks made a considerable amount of smoke and in the latter stages great care was needed not to set the malting on fire. Such malt definitely had no diastatic power but by the late 18th century Porter was made with a mixture of Brown and other paler malts. The latter provided the fermentable extract as it had the carefully preserved amylase enzymes.

There is also an issue about the temperatures Combrune recorded. It seems unlikely that malt would be turned brown in the hour or so he quotes or black by the time it was at 210°F. He doesn't state he was using degrees Fahrenheit but as Celsius had not been introduced and to this day is not common among British brewers and maltsters and the Fahrenheit thermometer had been recently invented, we must assume he was recording in those units. In addition, 48°C (119°F) does seem a reasonable temperature for finishing white malt even if the other temperatures he supplies don't really seem to stack up.

I assume that the heat applied by Combrune produced a temperature considerably higher than that he measured. The latent heat of vapourisation keeps the temperature within the body of malt much lower than the ambient temperature. This would explain why his brown malt was probably only brown on the outside. The centre remained much cooler. The diastatic power of the centre may in fact have remained somewhat protected and provided for some extract!

Combrune summarises 1750s malting temperatures thus:

Degrees	Colour	Malt Description	Maturation time (grow bright by precipitation)
119	White	White malt	2 weeks
124	W,W,Y	White turning to a light yellow	1 month
129	WWYY	Light yellow inclining to amber	2 months
134	WWYYR	Amber	4 months
138	WWYYRR	High amber or first brown	3 months
143	YYRR	Brown	4 months
148	YYRR	Middling brown	6 months
152	YRR	High brown	12 months
157	YRRB	Brown inclining to black.	18 months
162	YRRBB	High brown speckled with black.	2 years
167	RRBB	Blackish brown with red specks.	
171	RBB	Coffee colour	
176	Black	Black	

The whole Combrune exercise seems very unreliable and although he attracted much criticism he also enjoyed a pivotal role in the science of 18th century brewing. To give a maturation time dependent on malt colour instead of OG (original wort gravity prior to pitching) seems bizarre, but Porters were we believe brewed strong and kept long and Combrune seems to verify this. We have to remember that attempts to rationalise empiricism produced some bizarre hypothesise. Relationships between seemingly unconnected variables were postulated and tested using the new skills we call mathematics and science.

Some twenty years before Combrune there appeared the first of many reprints on malt in the *London & Country Brewer*. Early editions are without author but they are in fact the work of a man called William Ellis, a farmer. In the following pages I have virtually reprinted everything Ellis says about brown beer brewing, including making brown malt. From this it is clear that it *was* the intention to dry malt properly before it went to the kiln. But he does highlight the problems of the time of keeping the drying malt at a steady temperature and so it seems much malt was dried too fast. This causes the malt to become hard and glassy and eventually produces crystal malt, or if the heat is raised slowly, brown malt.

Combrune's description of wet malt at temperatures high enough to burn it may well have been something of a commonplace for brown malt makers. I suggest taking wet malt, driving all the surface water off at around 50°C (122°F) measured in the body of the malt, and then finishing it at 68-71°C (155-160°F) until quite brown on the outside only but in no way charred. It should be quite dry in the centre. This would also be close to the description 100 years after Combrune. The problem remains the firing material. Anthracite was the choice in the 18th century. Coke became a by-product of the 19th century chemical industry and was needed for town gas production. Its introduction relieved the transport problems associated with anthracite and its availability only in South Wales. Coke was made *in situ* where it was needed but anthracite and coke were by no means the universal choice in making brown malt even 100 years after Combrune. We shall see that the late 19th century still had room for an individual quality in brown malt, which certainly produced individual Stouts and Porters. Start drying those faggots!

1.3 HOPS AND THE 1750s

Combrune also gives us some hopping rates for Porters. However we know very little about the hops at his disposal. His description is then difficult to quantify.

"The quantity of hops, necessary for the preserving of pale beers, has been observed to be one pound weight to every quarter of malt, for every month the liquor is intended to be kept; but hops employed for these pale strong drinks are supposed to be new and strong, whereas, Porter, where the price does not keep an equal pace with the value of the commodity, hops, rather less in quality are thought to be sufficient.

Their quantity is, on this account, increased from 12 to 14 pound, per quarter."

This economical attitude to hops seems to have been common and to be fair, if only or predominantly brown malt were used in a Porter then a delicate hop flavour wasn't really needed. He is much more generous with hops than Ellis who recommended 3 pounds per 11 bushels. This works out at 5 ½ times Ellis' rates. Ellis often erred to much lower rates than that, at one point going as low as 1 lb per hogshead or roughly 1 lb per 10 bushels.

I've had to piece Combrune's method together from various snippets throughout his book. For example he gives the following information on brew lengths but in every piece of information there is a crucial element missing. In this table it is the malt type! Empirical brewing starts to lose its charm. Every brewer had his method, based on experience and would continue to use it, with or without Combrune's input. It is equally difficult to know by how much Combrune was influenced by brewers further afield than his home town. He certainly did not keep abreast of Farmer Ellis' thoughts in the *London & Country Brewer.*

Minimum length Barrels	Maximum length Barrels	Quarters malt	Beer type
4¼	4¼	1	Keeping small beer
4¾	5½	1	Amber or pale
1½	1¾	1	Brown strong or Porter
2¼	2¾	1	Burton ale

Again we see Combrune was trying to rationalise brewing. He linked all sorts of diverse parameters to each other and if one had the patience one could workout the conditioning time required by looking at the finishing temperature of the malting process. His links are very difficult to comprehend, but because he was published by the Worshipful Company of Brewers, there were certainly practicing brewers up and down the country who took note of what we perceive as ramblings. In fact he may not have been at the forefront of thinking in Porter brewing, but merely passing on established empirical wisdom. This needs further research!

The spirit of the age was to apply rational thought to problems and Combrune was obviously trying to be part of that scene. Viewed from the 21st century he seems downright bizarre but the 18th century is not there to be judged from our norms. Hart-Davis reminds us that 100 years after Combrune, the Belgian statistician Adolphe Quetelet published his law of flowering plants. Hart-Davis summarises the theory thus: "Counting from the last frost, common lilac flowers when the sum of the squares of the mean temperatures equals 4264 square degrees Centigrade."

It seriously shows how desperate people were to find scientific reasons for cause and effect. Maybe the lilac calculation is true, but who would care nowadays? In the 21st Century we want useful relationships between variables; relationships that will tell us if a plane will fly or a ship will float. The 18th century scientist was still struggling to decide what was important. By comparison with flowering lilac, Combrune seems quite sane for merely looking for the relationship between colour and enzyme activity in the cask. The much quoted Flemish chemist Boerhaave in his book *Elements of Chemistry vol 1 Essay on brewing* (1758) makes clear that one believed the alcohol to be already present in the barley and to be released during beer making. The combustible material in barley and malt was the alcohol but only by brewing could one release it usefully. We mustn't mock! Boerhaave's hypothesis explained the available evidence of the time and in the absence of further data must be considered good scientific reasoning. He seems to have had considerable influence over Combrune and certainly Porter brewing generally.

So it seems that a Combrune Porter may have looked like this:

RECIPE 1. HISTORICAL.

COMBRUNE'S STRONG BROWN BEER 1750

Combrune's Stout Beer after Harwood
Combrune dried his malt at 85°C (188°F). This would produce dark malt but by no means black. He doesn't seem to have pre-dried it at around 30-40°C (86-104°F), which would be common today. After thorough drying we finish the malt for colour at around 85°C (185°F).

Original Gravity	Not known			
Water: Anything available	25 litres	23 litres	5 UK gals	5 US gals
Brown malt	10.6 kg	9.8 kg	23.4 lb	19.0 lb
Copper hops	Goldings Maximum 5% alpha-acid.			
	500g	450g	16.7 oz	13.5 oz

Brewing method:
- First mash at 63°C (144°F). No time given but probably 1½-2 hours.
- Second mash 72°C (162°F). No time given but probably no more than 1 hour.
- Ferment right out, keg and mature for at least 3 months. If we work from his table, high brown was matured for 1 year.

- Comments:
- The hop quantities are awesome and as I assume the extract was mainly colour and browned starch this must have been a truly bitter beer. Combrune certainly didn't use his best hops for such a dark beer as he felt it unlikely he could recoup the cost in the price he could expect per barrel.
- We cannot guess the alcohol content as we have to doubt his malt descriptions. If indeed the malt was not brown right through, (e.g. middle or high brown) we may assume that there was plenty of colour and a fair bit of fermentable extract.
- This type of recipe would certainly have produced a beer close to the 18th century description of Porter, "dark, strong and bitter".

1.4 A MORE RATIONAL APPROACH

Even though Combrune received the backing of the Worshipful Company of Brewers, his grasp of brewing theory left much to be desired. We shouldn't think that he was at the forefront of English Porter. Much of what he wrote appears to us now to be arrant nonsense and this is all the more surprising as the *London & Country Brewer* of 1736 shows that many brewers had quite a firm grasp of brewing practice, even if they didn't fully understand the theory. But this was the age of empiricism and poor practice based on poor observations in one area of the country would not necessarily impact on all Porter brewers. Or maybe our writer Ellis (referred to blandly as "A Farmer") had the economic clout to get into print but not the birthright to mix it with the gentry. It may remain a mystery why Combrune enjoyed such credibility. Perhaps Ellis and Combrune didn't know of each other's existence. We do know that in an age where birthright was everything, a rich man and certainly a nobleman had no need for scientific reason to back up his opinions. Perhaps more research is needed into Combrune's connections among the mighty and rich.

Nevertheless Ellis delivers a description of drying brown malt similar to Combrune, and the same method was repeated well into the 19th century. He writes "There are several methods used in drying of Malts, the Iron-Plate frame, the Tyle-frame, that are both full of little holes: The Brass wyred and Iron wyred ; the Iron and tyled one, were chiefly invented for the drying of brown Malts and saving of fuel, for these when they come to be thorough-hot will make the corns crack and jump by the fierceness of their heat , so that they will be roasted or scorch'd in a little time."

Water was sprinkled on the hot malt, presumably to make it swell and give less weight for volume, but this obviously led to quicker deterioration. More important is the report, "Such hasty dryings or scorchings are also apt to bitter the malt by burning its skin and therefore these kilns are not so much used now as formerly." The description of the constitution of brown malt is quite similar to that described by Combrune. "The brown Malt is the soonest and highest dried of any, even till it is so hard, that it is difficult to bite some of its Corn asunder, and is often so crusted or burnt that the farinaceous part loses a great deal of its essential Salts and vital Property, which frequently deceives the ignorant Brewer, that hopes to draw as much Drink from a quarter of this as he does from pale or amber sorts."

Amber malt receives great praise as being "free of either extreme" (pale or brown). "Its colour pleasant, its taste agreeable and its nature wholesome."

While amber malt could be mashed with either hard or soft liquor or a mixture of both, beers from brown malt had to be mashed with soft

Thames water or "New River Water". By this I assume he means water that is freshly rained off the land and not spring water, which would have dissolved salts in it. "It makes a luscious Ale for a little while, and a But-beer that will keep well five or six Months but after that time it generally grows stale, notwithstanding there being ten to twelve bushels allowed to the Hogshead and it be hopp'd accordingly".

I mention this because it is generally accepted that the original name for Porter was "Entire Butt", sometimes written "Intire". I am sure though that But-beer was just a description for a dark beer brewed for keeping in a *Butt*. The spellings *But-Beer* and *Intire* should not irritate us. Spelling was an irrelevancy to many 18th century writers. More irritating is trying to sort out when a brown beer was a butt beer, or intire butt or Porter or even Stout. The naming is so mixed and so irrelevant to writers and brewers of the time that I have lost the will to believe the Harwood – pot of three threads – Porter story. Protz (*Classic Stout & Porter* 1997) has a photo of a painting, showing a Whitbread pub, advertising London Porter and Whitbread Entire. Unfortunately a fine lamp obscures the name of the pub and Protz, in his infuriating style supplies neither date, painter nor source. Protz believes it to prove that Porter and Entire were two separate brown beers, presumably as late as 1800.

The drying fuel for malt was, by 1736, already culm out of choice. "straw, wood and fern are apt to give the malt an offensive tang…." If culm wasn't available, pit coal was burned sufficiently to remove all the sulphur and other volatiles and then used to provide the finest pale malts. Culm (coal from Swansea which we would now call anthracite) was preferred and burnt cleanly enough for direct use in malting, but this fuel was in strong demand for converting chalk into lime for agriculture. Thus it was that straw was taken if culm or coke were not to be got and wood and fern were a last resort. In both the 1736 and 1744 editions of the *London & Country Brewer* we find the same quote, and this is a key to early 18th century dark beers.

"Brown malts are dried with Straw, Wood and Fern, etc. The Straw-dried is far the best, but the Wood-sort has a most unnatural Taste, that few can bear with it, but the Necessitous, and those that are accustomed to its strong smoaky Tang; yet it is much used in some of the Western Parts of England, and many thousand Quarters of this Malt have been formerly used in London for brewing the Butt-keeping Beers with, and that because it sold for two Shillings per quarter cheaper than the Straw-dried malt; nor was this Quality of the Wood-dried Malt much regarded by some of its Brewers, for that its ill Taste is lost in nine or twelve months, by the Age of the Beer, and the Strength of the great Quantity of Hops that were used in its Preservation.

"The Fern-dried malt is also attended with a rank disagreeable Taste from the Smoak of this Vegetable, with which many Quarters of Malt are dried, as appears by the great quantities annually cut by our

Maltsters on our Commons, for the two prevalent Reasons, Cheapness and Plenty".

This gives another reason for Porter being stored so long; to relieve the drinker of the over-powering presence of the wood smoke.

I'm afraid that a genuine 18th century brown malt looks beyond our 21st century means and with it goes hope of a Porter brewed from it! This is no bad thing. Consider the amounts of black or chocolate malt we would nowadays include as colouring and taste in a modern Porter or Stout. Would we consider making a Brown Beer from only such malt, and then hopping it fearfully to give it keeping qualities? I doubt it and I doubt we would want to drink it.

But it *was* popular stuff. Pope wrote in 1775,

"Lo! The poor toper whose untutored sense,
Sees bliss in ale, and can with wine dispense,
Whose head proud fancy never taught to steer,
Beyond the muddy ecstasies of beer."

Muddy it must have been, black as night and like burnt toast and the country loved it! Interestingly the wine trade has turned the tables on us beer lovers. It took over 200 years but Pope has certainly got his wish. Traditional beers have never been so unfashionable and wine is certainly the drink of the moment.

So what malt to use for an early 18th century Stout beer? I think malt carefully dried and then finished in the kiln at 100°C (212°F) could well be used entirely for a dark beer. It may not be dark enough, although kilning times in excess of 10 hours do produce a wonderfully dark beer! Imperial malt was finished at 130°C (298°F) for several hours. Thus I recommend taking a good sample of pale malt and giving it 5 hours at 130°C (298°F) in a fan oven. At the end of the day you will have to decide yourself how dark you want your Stout beer to be. The idea must be to preserve some of the white corn substance and only scorch the outside of the grain. The black colour and burnt flavour of Combrune's Stout may not find favour anymore and just be regarded as a historical novelty, best left undrunk, but it remains a good way of finishing up old hops.

1.5 EMPIRICAL MASHING TECHNIQUES

Chapter 11 of the *London & Country Brewer 1736* gives us an insight into mashing at that time. The chapter is entitled "*A philosophical Account for Brewing Strong October Beer. By an Ingenious Hand*". I paraphrase.

- The malt was left at least two months in a heap to prove, a procedure, which would certainly be avoided now. Modern malts come off the wire and straight into a plastic bag, where they are kept sealed from the air. The feeling was that the corn substance from a malt held in air "dissolved easier in the mash". This maybe true, but we now consider it would be to the detriment of the beer. Malt drying was done according to the darkness of the intended beer. High dried malts were crushed to a much bigger particle size than pale malts. The aim was to keep the husk as whole as possible as it was considered detrimental to the beer if tiny ground up particles were able to leave the draff, and be carried through with the wort. Fierce acidic fermentations were thought to be the result of husk reaching the boil. Nowadays we would certainly not expect husk to be carried from the draff but we do take care not to sparge too hot as some brewers allege this causes some unpleasant side tastes.
- Once the malt was ground it was left another day to prove before being used. This too was thought to improve the solubility of the kernel.
- The mash liquor was prepared somewhat unusually for our understanding, but this technique was widespread well into the 19th century. The liquor was brought to the boil with the addition of a few handfuls of hops. The mash liquor temperature was then reduced to the strike temperature by adding cold water. The strike temperature was just cool enough not to scald the hand (or the malt). Mature weathered washing-up hands can cope with temperatures up to 70°C (158°F) before scalding occurs and so we see empiricism triumphs without a thermometer.
- The hot wort was run from the malt into the underback through a bed of hops as this prevented the beer blinking or becoming foxed.
- Running off and boiling the worts was also carefully defined. Clearest worts were obtained by running the wort out slowly, hence the need for the disinfecting power of the hops.
- The first wort run off was boiled quickly and vigorously, the second for longer and the third longest. No times are given

except for the first boil where 1½ hours is recommended. That said it all depended on the hot break occurring and the hops were not boiled above 30 minutes. Providing this 30-minute rule was adhered to the brewer could use two or even three times the normal amount of hops without risking harshness or off flavours.

- Sparging was thought to be unknown until the first half of the 19th century when it was developed in Scotland. English brewers were reluctant to switch over to sparging and continued with the more cumbersome multiple mash technique. The original meaning of the term mashing was "stirring". Over the years it has come to replace the terms stirring *and* extraction of the malt substance with water by infusion. Hence, when we talk of mashing in the 18th century we really mean stirring with aliquots of water. So the first strong wort was run off and a new charge of hotter water added to the grist. Again the wisdom had been accumulated that said running very hot liquor onto the grist leads to problems with side tastes, caused we now know by phenols and dextrins being washed through, which are much less soluble in cooler water.

- Yeast starters were not needed as by and large one only had access to a working yeast. Nevertheless the 18th century brewer understood that the yeast should be introduced carefully to the wort, presumably avoiding sudden temperature changes and introducing the cells to a new medium by giving them time to adjust. So the yeast was added in small amounts to the wort and left unstirred. This allowed any dead cells to settle immediately. Once the viable cells showed signs of life and activity, they were whisked into the wort. This process was repeated until the wort was fermented out. This technique eventually became what we now understand under "rousing". This puts oxygen into the wort to help cell reproduction and prevents viable cells being taken to the bottom of the fermenter by the waste solids and dead cells.

- The lees were "thrown on the malt to mend a small beer."

Interestingly Porter is never referred to as a drink in the 1736 edition of *London & Country Brewer*, although the usage of the word for a strong bitter dark beer must date from around that time. Brown Ale and Stout are frequently mentioned and considerable detail is available to us on how to mash a brown beer, in the "Country or Private way of Brewing." Stout as a term only referred to the strength and colour of the beer, but we mustn't forget that strength and colour were inseparable in the minds of the 18th century brewer. So a Brown Beer was a dark beer of moderate strength and Stout a stronger version in terms of bushels per barrel of malt and pounds per barrel of hops. I find the following London Stout to be very moderately hopped, but being a 100% brown malt gyle there wasn't much point in wasting good hops on it.

RECIPE 2. HISTORICAL.

EXTRA STRONG LONDON STOUT (LONDON & COUNTRY 1736 SECTION 38).

London 40/- Stout Beer.

This particular gyle was made in a 2-bushel mash tun. Even for the early 18th century this was a modest amount to make in one batch. A bushel is around 8 gallons of corn, which I calculate would be about 20 kg. This is twice the capacity of what most Craft Brewers work with nowadays and so is quite relevant to us.

The use of London river water is handy for home-brewers in the capital. Much domestic water in the Thames Valley comes from the river. It is no longer stagnant and full of red worms, which was a common 18th century problem and makes a little bit of chlorine sound a small price to pay. London river and well waters were fairly high in carbonate hardness. We are told that if any person within a London brewhouse used the word "water" instead of the brewer's term "liquor" they would pay a sixpence forfeit. That would be nearly 5 pints of strong beer.

We are short on detail for this brew. The values given would be for a brew "sold at 30/- from the tun." We are not told what the final volume of this 2 bushel brew was, but only that it sold for 40/- wholesale, so the malt amounts given must be seen as the very minimum used. This was all brown malt!

Original Gravity	Not known			
London River or well Water	25 litres	23 litres	5 UK gals	5 US gals
Brown malt	21.3 kg	19.6 kg	46.8 lb	37.9 lb
Copper hops	Goldings Maximum 5% alpha-acid.			
	44g	41g	1.5 oz	1.2 oz

Brewing method:

First stiff mash.

- Bring the first liquor nearly to the boil with a good covering of malt husks to accelerate the process.
- Part the malt and test the temperature of the liquor. It must be just endured without causing blistering.
- Run enough cold water onto the liquor to bring it to just above blood heat.
- Run the liquor up through the false bottom of the mash tun into the malt.
- Mash the goods for 30 minutes.

Second mash.

- Set a new liquor charge heating, this time to boiling point.
- Turn off the heat and when it has ceased boiling run it onto the goods. The temperature should rise to around 62-66°C (142-150°F).
- Mash well and cover the goods with a good layer of malt.
- Stand for 1 hour.
- Run the wort off into the underback and boil for 90 minutes with the hops.

Fermentation

- Cool the wort, strain and pitch the yeast at around 35°C (95°F). It should ferment out in around 2 ½ days.
- These low hopping rates were for a beer to be kept 1-3 weeks before being tapped. A keeping Stout beer (3 months in the cask) had three times the above hopping rates.

Comments:

- The hopping rates quoted here are extremely low. It was common practice to cover liquor being prepared or the goods in the mash tun with a good layer of malt, which acted as insulation. I have adopted the practice of covering the goods with about 2cm of pale malt for this purpose. This is in addition to the mash tun lid.
- The pitching temperature is very high, but was probably done for convenience as well as safety. This was a winter brew and the brewhouse was certainly very cold. Pitching the yeast warm got the fermentation off to a flyer. As the wort cooled slowly down to 15°C (59°F) it was protected by a good layer of working yeast and blanket of carbon dioxide. The sin and error of fermenting too warm was well understood. Only cheap beers were fermented at "blood heat", for (they pitch and) "carry it away the very next Morning early to their customers, who commonly draw it out in less than a weeks time."
- Cool fermentations helped a beer keep. Amber and pale ales would take a week to ferment and the wort "beaten several times for the better incorporating the Yeast with the Wort". We would now refer to this as "rousing".
- All brewers used an active yeast sample from a previous brew. This was added along with a considerable quantity of beer and it appears that aerating the wort was not necessary. The addition of air by rousing probably helped the yeast produce new viable cells and so kept the strain in better condition.

1.6 THE COUNTRY OR PRIVATE WAY OF BREWING. (ELLIS 1736)

"The Country or private way of Brewing" refers to economies of scale. The town breweries were already making beer in quantities which would humble arrogant 21st century man, who generally believes that without roads, rail, modern farming and computer control, things must have looked very primitive. Consider information from the Doomsday Book, written after the 1066 invasion of England by the Norman King William the Conquerer. William was rather unsure what actually belonged to him and so he sent his scribes far and wide in the new Kingdom and told them to record, and that is what they did and the results of their labours can still be seen in the British Museum in London.

From this source we know that the Monks of St. Paul's in London brewed 1884 barrels of ale from

175 quarters of barley, 175 quarters wheat and 708 quarters oats.

This is 66 368 gallons from 355 488 lbs grain, which I calculate as about 21lbs per 5 US or 4 imperial gallons.

Maybe their methodology looks primitive but the ingenuity of brewers past in overcoming obstacles makes me realise in what a dependency culture we now live!

The town brewer also had purpose built utensils at his disposal and was not likely to be distracted by other occupations such as getting the harvest in. "But the private brewer is not without his benefits; for he can have his malt ground at pleasure, his tubs and moveable Coolers sweeter and better cleaned than the great fixed Tuns and Backs, he can skim off his yeast and leave his bottom leas behind, which is what the great Brewers can't so well do; he can at discretion make additions of cold wort to his too forward Ales and Beers….." Sounds like Craft Brewing to me!

It would not surprise me to find it was the country brewer who discovered the truth about malt. Although Stout beers, (later to be called Porter) were brewed truly black there is no doubt that some brewers were already aware of the economic folly of this practice. Again it is the *London and Country Brewer* of 1736 which tells us, "The pale malt is the slackest dried of any, and where it has a leisure fire, a sufficient time allowed in the kiln, and a due care taken of it , the flower of the grain will remain in its full quantity, and thereby produce a greater length of wort than the brown high dried Malt, for which reason it is sold for one or two shillings a quarter more than that: This pale malt is also the most nutritious sort to the body of all others, as being in the state most simple and nearest to its Original Barley Corn that will retain its Alcalous and Balsamick quality much longer than the brown sort; the tender drying of this Malt bringing its body into so softer texture of Parts, that most of the great Brewers, brew it with Spring and Well-waters, whose hard and binding Properties they think agrees best with this loose-bodied Malt, either in Ales or Beers, and which will also dispense with hotter waters in brewing of it, than the brown Malt can".

Our writer holds forth with the way the ignorant brewer is often deceived into believing that he will draw as much extract from brown malts as he does from others. He also reports that the occasional brewer was a hundred years ahead of his time and already using a technique closer to 1830 than 1730. "At Bridport in Dorsetshire, I knew an Innkeeper use half Pale and half Brown malt for Brewing his Butt-beers, that proved to my Palate the best I ever drank on the Road, which I think may be accounted for, in that Pale being the slackest, and the Brown the hardest dryed, must produce a mellow good Drink by the help of the requisite Age, that will reduce those extremes to a proper Quality".

This Bridport gyle was already the beginning of the end for all brown malt beers.

RECIPE 3. HISTORICAL.

STRONG BUTT-BEER (LONDON & COUNTRY 1736 SECTIONS 22 & 43).

Bridport Butt Beer.

This good brewer of Dorsetshire seems not to have given much away, but the fact that his Butt-beers were made with Pale malt. This was common later in the 19th century and Amsinck still made the distinction between country and town Porters as late as 1850, although no Porter or Stout was commercially made with all brown malt. There is reason to believe that 19th century brown malt was darker than that described by Combrune and the addition of Pale malt became a necessity.

In the absence of Bridport-detail I have taken the brewing method from the "Country or private way of Brewing". This is a distillation by the London & Country Brewer of several methods known to him from Wales, Dorchester Nottingham, Oundle, "and many other places", which the writer asserts will serve the London private brewer too.

Original Gravity	Not known			
Hard well water	25 litres	23 litres	5 UK gals	5 US gals
Brown malt	6.5 kg	6 kg	14.5 lb	12 lb
Pale malt	6.5 kg	6 kg	14.5 lb	12 lb
Copper hops	Goldings Maximum 5% alpha-acid.			
	132g	120g	4.5 oz	3.6 oz

Brewing method:

First stiff mash.

- Bring the first liquor nearly to the boil with a good covering of malt husks to accelerate the process.
- Ladle both the liquor and husks into the mash tun and allow to cool until you can see your face clearly in the liquor.
- Run the malt in slowly, keeping a pound back. Stir during the addition to prevent balling occurring.
- This should be a genuinely stiff mash.
- Use the remaining malt to cover the goods.
- Rest the mash 2 to 3 hours.

Second mash.

- Set a new liquor charge heating, this time to boiling point.
- Set the tap and run off a small amount of wort and replace it with near boiling water from the boiler.

This process was repeated until the correct quantity of wort was achieved for a particular beer or the copper was full. This took up to 15 hours.

A second mash was used in addition to the washing if a thinner beer was required.

Boiling

- Put 30g (1oz) hops in a muslin bag. (Canvas was the 18th century choice) and boil in the wort for 30 minutes. Replace the hops with a second aliquot and boil for another 30 minutes. Repeat this one more time so a total boil of 90 minutes is achieved. For a keeping beer it seems the spent hops may not have been removed before the next addition.

Fermentation

- Ferment out in the way described in recipe 2.

Comments:

- If no small beer was made from a previous mash then the second running was used as the first liquor for the next brew.
- The malt was added to the liquor when one could just see one's face in the liquor. A cold brewery steamed up very quickly but a time came when the intensity of the condensing steam coming off the liquor was sufficiently diminished to allow the brewer to see his reflection in the liquor surface. I assume this was around 75°C (167°F) in a winter brewery and was a commonly used temperature measurement before thermometers became easily available.
- The Oundle way of brewing demanded that the wort was run off in a "stream as thin as straw". This wort was replaced with near boiling water, the in and outputs being kept balanced. This accounted for the long sparge process of up to 15 hours, for this was surely the beginning of sparging, a process normally attributed to the Scottish Brewers one hundred years later.

The "Country way of brewing," has one more surprise for us and a technique quite lost in the sands of time. The use of malts dried as strongly as brown malt must have given rise to some very powerfully tasting Stouts. It appears that the sharpest flavours could be removed with active charcoal. Charcoal has an incredibly high surface area and the ability to bond organic molecules to it. It is still commonly used as a decolourising agent by organic chemists and Schnapps burners let their distillate run through charcoal to get rid of the taste of burnt malt caused by hot spots in the still. Small family brewers dunked burnt toast into beer with off flavours and this seems to have been a practice prevalent well into the late 19th century. Betsy Trotwood dunked toast in her Ale (*David Copperfield*). Burnt toast is bread covered in a layer of active charcoal and according to the *London & Country Brewer* of 1736 it was common practice to use this technique to lessen the burnt or wood-smoke flavour in Stouts made from 100% brown malt. This was done during the mash and it wasn't necessary to buy the charcoal the way we could do now. If the copper was fired with coal then some red hot burning cinders were taken, covered in salt which apparently lessened the effect of sulphur in the coal and these cinders were plunged deep into the dry malt, just before the liquor was run in, or into the wetted goods during the mash. Brewers with wood fired boilers quenched one or more of the burning ends in a copper of wort "to mellow the drink as burnt toast of bread does a pot of beer; but it is to be observed, that this must not be done with Oak, Firr, or any other strong-scented Wood, lest it does more harm than good."

1.7 PORTER, DIALECTICAL MATERIALISM AND THE CHANGE IN NAME

The industrial revolution was studied at length by one Karl Marx. He gave us the theory of economics driven by the dialectic. He studied many economic situations but never Porter, which is a shame for Porter was the drink that changed like a chameleon in order to meet the economic realities of brewing in the 18th and 19th centuries.

In the 1736 tract by Ellis there is no mention of the word "Porter". Mathias records that the full 1734-38 *London & Country Brewer* collection does have a mashing method for Porter, although in the edition I have it is referred to as Butt-Beer. Certainly the 1750 edition tells us how to mash Porter, but more importantly allows us to link it to earlier editions. In Chapter 10 we find "Of Brewing Butt-Beer, now called Porter." So maybe Ellis was a traditionalist and didn't use the new word until much later in his career. It appears that Butt-Beer was Porter was old-fashioned Brown Beer and the name changed to suit the economic advantage to be gained.

Certainly the word Porter occurs as early as 1729 (Oxford Dictionary) and Harwood is attributed with having brewed the first Porter in Shoreditch in 1722. He didn't call it Porter but entire butts, and it may have taken a few years for the name to become established.

It is also important to know that for a beer so talked about but so little drunk for the last hundred years, its introduction to the brewing public was as big a watershed in the history of brewing, as was the introduction of hops. The introduction of hops at least created a qualitative change in the beer, but the introduction of Porter may have been a straight marketing ploy. Like hops it was economic pressures, which secured Porter as the beer of the eighteenth century. Hops were condemned to succeed because of their anti-bacterial properties. Porter was condemned to succeed because it could be brewed in any weather, unlike ale, which could not be brewed during the hottest months of the year in any quantity. If Porter tasted good when all other young (and thereby cheaper) beers were struggling with the weather, then the dark beer was always going to be the punter's choice.

The reason for Porter's (and other brown beer's) tolerance to warm weather brewing is that a fermentation process is quite exothermic and large fermentation vats could only really lose the heat released by the fermentation, through the surface of the liquid. If the fermentation vat was covered to prevent the beer becoming foxed, less heat escaped and so the fermentation went faster and produced more heat. Ales regularly foamed out the fermentation vat. If the poor beleaguered brewer roused the beer after uncovering the vessel, which was also common practice, he moved in more air, encouraged infection and the aerobic fermentation, which releases twenty-five times as much heat as the alcoholic anaerobic fermentation. Furthermore most beer is drunk in hot weather at the very time one can't brew it. This regularly led to shortages, which could not be easily tolerated. For example, the Navy was most active in the summer months and often had to suffer sour beer on board. Imagine tying up in London in mid-July after months, or maybe years at sea and finding no beer to drink in the whole town. The sailors were very reluctant members of the King's Navy anyway, and probably had been pressed into service by use of tricks, villainy and violence. The Admiralty knew it had to get beer for these men if uncomfortable and dangerous confrontations were to be avoided, and would commission breweries to brew no matter how ill advised the undertaking would be.

The dark brown Porter wort, made from brown malt, fermented more gently than ale and as such was more suited to large volume production in warm weather. Large-scale beer production was essential to supply the needs of the new emerging industrial cities and bodies such as the King's Navy and without attemperators, which had to wait for the ingenuity of the 19th century Porter was the only large scale way forward

One may think that it would have been difficult to find a market for a "new beer" and that the drinking public would reject Porter, which was, after all, a beer of convenience to the trade, but it had at that time long been common practice to mix beers in the ale house. This was primarily done because many beers didn't keep well, so if one barrel needed using it would be mixed in the glass with a fresher sample in order to bring the hardened beer up to an acceptable taste. Perhaps the reverse was true too. A properly matured beer may have been stretched a little to cover some which were rather young. Some mixtures became popular and so would be ordered out of preference. A Brown Mixed is still common in Liverpool as was a Mild and Bitter in London. Entire Butts (later Porter) was maybe made popular to the drinker by *claiming* it had been brewed especially to imitate a frequently requested mixture and to that end, a special Porter malt had been kilned. Complete non-sense of course. We know the same beer had been brewed for decades and sold as Brown Beer. Sure publicans mixed beers in order to mask a bad one or lengthen a well-matured beer with some cheap young ones, but let's not fool ourselves with the idea that entire butts was a special brew, which was a genuine imitation of the mixture. Anyone who has brewed extensively knows it just doesn't happen like that. An all brown malt beer should taste the same as a random mixture from an equally random publican's cellar? Please!

Sure the publicans were easy to win over too! It is certain that pub-licans found it a considerable nuisance to run to three barrels to mix one drink, (unless they had a poor quality beer to hide) and they were happy to introduce Porter as a solution. So on two fronts, brewer and publi-can, marketing entire butts was a godsend. I imagine the drinker was a willing convert too. The drinker had been used to mixtures designed to cover the shortcomings of one or more of the components. If Harwood brewed a decent brown beer and didn't adulterate it with rogue ones, it's hardly surprising the drinker noticed an improvement!

And so to Harwood! Myth has it that Harwood, of the Bell Brewhouse in Shoreditch, was the first to brew a brown beer to replace the mixtures so common at the time. In 1722 Harwood is supposed to have called his creation "entire butts". The evidence for this story is next to nothing and yet it is quoted as being gospel truth. Harwood existed as did the Bell and entire butts, but thereafter we are into myth. I can find no evidence of the link.

The drink called entire butts became so popular that in the sixty or so years after the introduction of a brown beer, specifically brewed for quality and not to mix with other lesser beers, that all sorts of mild amber and brown ales, many known as Porter, came on the market. The publican was happy to avoid the leg-work involved in mixing an order, and to make the most of the popular demand this beer enjoyed. The drinker noticed an improvement in the beer, for it had not been mixed with other doubtful quality barrels. And this also explains the fact that later Porters had everything but the kitchen sink thrown in. Oddball recipes containing peppers, capsicum, ginger and liquorice were com-mon. Surely these were attempts to make a Porter tasting beer without the hassle of making brown malt or running to three taps, and it also justifies or rubbishes the modern Porter styles that are defined for com-petitions. All these beers were Porter to someone and all our modern day recreations surely have a historical precedent somewhere. Is there such a thing as a genuine "style"? A know-all beer judge will say yes and bang on about colour and hopping rates. A historian will say you can enter anything in the competition! Someone somewhere has brewed it and called it Porter!

There is another Porter myth, which needs investigating. If mixtures were used to cover the taste of a beer past its sell-by date, did the drinker come to expect the stale beer taste? Protz (*Classic Porter & Stout* 1997) suggest the stale sour taste was desirable and special backs were constructed, into which brown beer was pumped to allow it to acetify and give it the lactic taste and Korzonas (*Homebrewing* 1997) says it was inevitable that any beer conditioned in wooden casks would be the victim of the brettanomyces fungus. I doubt both ideas. Protz doesn't supply convincing sources. I just can't believe that the bulk of beer drinkers would prefer to drink a lactic bitten beer in preference to a clean one. I have deliberately staled beers to test the theory. Drinkable? Maybe. Desirable? Never!!! The brewing literature of the 18th and 19th centuries abounds with methods for curing a "foxed beer". (Ellis *The London & Country Brewer* 1736). Ellis conceded that the wooden barrels presented problems in certain circumstances. I believe they were tarred if any question mark hung over their purity. When reading Ellis I am staggered at the accuracy of his empirical wisdom and I don't believe they *had* to put up with tainted beer. Yes, sour lactobacilli beer was drunk out of necessity, (it won't kill you), yes drinkers got used to it, but no! they never demanded it out of preference. All references I've found view infected beer as a calamity.

And the problems with wild yeast infection, whether brettanomyces or anything else, were ever present. Sometimes beers were doubtless ruined but I can find no evidence from taste descriptions of the time, that brettanomyces infection were either expected or wanted.

So if Harwood's contribution is unproven is Harwood's brown malt really essential? Yes, if you want a 1720s look-alike. But many brown beers used the name Porter and had next to no brown malt at all, especially in the 19th century.

What is the best evidence for the Harwood yarn? Perhaps the most rigorously researched book on this subject is by Mathias, (*Brewing Industry in England 1700-1830*). But even he hedges his bets on the Harwood Porter story, provides no sources and qualifies his statement with "apparently." Mathias says that Harwood's Porter (which he probably never called "Porter"), was a "black thick beer, bitter to the tongue," of greater apparent strength and nourishment than existing ales". It required a malt dried and then kilned at a higher temperature than was usual for ales and its name (Entire Butts by Harwood), is supposed to have indicated a replacement for a mixture of half ale and half beer (half and half). For the real connoisseurs there was a mixture of one-third ale, one third beer and one third twopenny, a so-called "pot of three threads" according to Bickerdyke, so the new brew saved a lot of legwork. Although Mathias claims Bickerdyke as the source for the Harwood story, he actually contradicts Bickerdyke by asserting Porter was stronger than other existing ales. Bickerdyke claims Porter was actually weaker than other Stout Beers and recounts that a mixture of Stout and weaker Porter was ordered under the name of "cooper". Now anyone who has read Bickerdyke will know he is the quintessential Victorian gossip. Can one believe anything he claims? There is only one other writer I've found who agrees with Bickerdyke's Pot of Three Threads come Harwood story and that is in *A treatise on brewing* by Morrice dated 1802. Eighty years after the event doesn't exactly qualify as contemporaneous and so the whole thing may be myth. Morrice recorded a yarn, Bickerdyke read and copied Morrice and no one wants to spoil a good story for the sake of a few white lies, so urban myth becomes cast iron truth. Ever since, it has generally been believed Harwood replaced the legwork by brewing a single decent brown beer, with no adulteration, and called it "Entire Butts". This name changed to "Porter" sometime within the next few years, but not at Harwood's behest. Nevertheless, Morrice provides such an excellent account of brewing in London from the 1700s onwards that he must be taken seriously. I include an extended extract from his 1802 edition in appendix 1.

The 1863 edition of *The Brewer* offers the same story, but also a much more plausible alternative. Harwood is supposed to have had his beer ported, or carried to his customers in pewter pots. His potboys cried "Porter" to announce themselves as they knocked on doors. This sounds much more likely and the beer they carried was Brown Beer or Stout, which received the name Porter. "There is the Porter at the door," ceased to be the lad and became the beer he carried. This story also removes all the myth about special malts for special beers. That was surely just marketing hype! Maybe Harwood was astute and realised that there was mileage in offering the customer something better than mixtures of beers, at least one of which wouldn't stand inspection, so he brewed one decent beer with brown malt and rightly told the customer that this was a genuine step in the right direction.

Why weren't other commodities such as fish, eggs or butter called Porter? It was common throughout the 18th and 19th centuries to have a dinner, with beer *ported*. This was a take-away delivery service, each pub serving the immediate neighbourhood only with fresh food and drink. Not even milk was delivered to the doorstep, but was sold from a central point in a square or on a street corner.

The change in usage of Butt-Beer to Porter could have happened. Harwood's name "Entire Butt" could easily have shifted to Ellis's Butt-Beer and if this became a favourite among the market workers and stevedores around Shoreditch then the name Porter may have been adopted for brown beer or entire butts. There is little evidence though, and the

Oxford Dictionary covers itself by writing, "(1727, Porter's beer is so called) *apparently* because originally made for porters and other labourers," and in so doing supplies us with another alternative version but one which we can certainly dispose with. The porters and labourers did not have the economic clout to get anyone to brew a beer at their behest. Chambers Twentieth Century Dictionary gives no dates but suggests (wisely) that the drink preceded the taste later developed for it by the labourers. There really is no evidence that Porter was brewed specially for market workers and the story only occurs in evidence dating from the 19th century. That may be the clue for it was common among middle class Victorians to romanticise the labours of the common man, wringing his living from the soil in a pre-industrial revolution paradise. This reached its most vulgar climax in Pre-Raphaelite paintings such as *The Stonebreaker* (Wallis 1857), *The Hireling Shepherd* (Hunt 1851) or *Christ in the House of his Parents* and *The Woodman's Daughter* (Millais 1851). They are charming enough if you like that sort of thing but have nothing to do with reality. I believe the *Porter brewed for labourers* yarn belongs in the same genre of Victorian silliness.

The only nearly contemporaneous reference to the name Porter linking to the labouring classes is delivered by Protz (*Classic Stout & Porter* 1997). He quotes one Obadiah Poundage, a London brewer in the middle of the 18th century. "…the labouring people, porters etc. experienced its wholesomeness and utility, they assumed to themselves the use thereof, from whence it was called Porter…" (1760). Unfortunately Protz doesn't reveal the source but to be fair to him, if I found a quote from a man named Obidiah Poundage I too would want it in my book! Protz also quotes the French writer De Saussere who substantiates the labourer story, but again no source. Shame!

Poundage seems a sound enough source; He was apparently a London brewer etc. except . . .

Willoughby (*Sense & Sensibility*) and Faujas (appendix 8) were gentlemen who drank Porter. 18th century England was very hide bound by class. I think it inconceivable that Jane Austen would have her hero drink a beverage named after labourers or that the Royal Society would have entertained a drink of such low parentage at one of their dinners.

What is of interest is Ellis' details for this new fangled beer, originally known as Butt-Beer but by 1750 re-christened "Porter" by him. We know Ellis was a farmer. He describes himself on the title page of the 1736 edition of the *London & Country Brewer*, "A person formerly concerned in a Common Brewhouse in *London*, but for 20 years has resided in the Country."

If the name "Porter" became common by 1729 in East London it is plausible that its spread to the rest of the country took many years. Perhaps it was the decentralised nature of England and poor communications, which launched Porter as the beer shrouded in mystery; the beer everyone drank but gets no one mentioned apart from in brewing journals. This could explain the absence of reference to "Porter" in the 1736 *London & Country Brewer*. But the 1736 edition contains references enough to Entire or Intire and to Butts and But beer. Evidence then that the words had been around at least since the beginning of the century and maybe Harwood was the one to join them together as Entire Butts.

The mystery surrounding Porter has not only survived for over 200 years but its myth has been enhanced during that time. The Grapes in Liverpool has a fine leaded glass window proclaiming the fine Porters sold within, but alas the window is certainly not more that 30 years old and was fitted at least 100 years after Porter had ceased to be brewed in any quantity in that city. I note this as an illustration of the sentimentality this beer has evoked not only in the 19th century, but also throughout the latter half of the 20th century, no doubt helped by the Irish folk music revival of the 60s and 70s. Great yarns, fantastic songs and lyrics, all urban myth and have nothing to do with Porter. More tragic is the probability that by the time this book goes to press, the fine window in The Grapes will have been consigned to the builder's skip as another beautiful Victorian pub building becomes a lager and fast food outlet. *

So what does Ellis' 1750 description of mashing Porter tell us? The method is not far removed from the 40/- London Stout recipe which was prevalent in the Capital at that time, and which Ellis suggested for general adoption throughout the country.

* By Autumn 2002 the fine window was indeed in a builder's skip. My daughter tried to purchase it for me, but the owners were not interested. It couldn't even be photographed, for it had been covered in posters for the last 12 months of its life.

RECIPE 4. HISTORICAL.

OF BREWING BUTT BEER, CALLED PORTER. (LONDON & COUNTRY BREWER 1750 CHAPTER 10 PP 221).

23/- Porter.

Even though this has close similarities to the London Butt Beer recipe of 1736 it was brewed much thinner and fetched a correspondingly lower price. This was an all-brown-malt gyle!

I have taken Ellis' original text and broken it down into steps. Otherwise these are all his words.

Original Gravity	Not known			
London River or well Water	25 litres	23 litres	5 UK gals	5 US gals
Brown malt	14.2 kg	13 kg	31lb	25 lb
Copper hops	Goldings Maximum 5% alpha-acid.			
	200g	180g	6.7 oz	5.4 oz

Brewing method:

Mashing

- The water just breaks or boils when they let in a Quantity of cold water to keep it from scalding, and up through a false bottom into the malt;
- Then mash with wooden oars half an hour; by this time the water in the copper is scalding hot, which they likewise let run into the malt; and mash half an hour longer.
- They cap and cover the fresh malt, and let it stand two hours; then spend away by a Cock-Stream into the underback, where it lies a little while, 'till a second liquor is ready to boil, but not boil, with which they mash again to have a sufficient length of wort that they boil at once, or twice according to the bigness of the utensils.
- Others will make a third mash, and boil a second copper of wort.

Boiling

- The first wort is allowed an hour and a half's boiling with three pounds of hops to each barrel. The second wort two hours with the same hops and so on.

Fermenting

- When in the right temper they let down the worts out of the backs into the Tun from their grosser contents, where they coolly ferment with yeast, 'till a fine culr'd head rises and just falls again, that sometimes requires twenty four, sometimes forty eight hours, as the Weather is hot or cold to perform this operation.

Racking

- They then cleanse it off into Barrels one day and carry it out the next to their Customers, keeping the Vessels filling up now and then in the interim.

Comments
- Some call the first, hop Wort and the second, mash Wort; the third Neighbour-Wort, and the fourth blue. Which last being a small sort is sometimes allowed six or seven hours boiling with the same used Hops.
- For making this Drink with a good body, they frequently draw off a Barrel and a Firkin, or a Hogshead, from a quarter of Brown Malt and sell it for twenty three shillings per Barrel. But this is governed by the price to the customer; so that two or three sorts are sometimes carried out from one brewing, for with the blue they can lower it at pleasure; always observing that the higher the malt is dried the cooler the first liquor must be taken and used; therefore the first wort governs the second liquor either to be hotter or cooler. If that was too hot you may know it by its bearing too great a head or froth in the receiver, and é Contra; a middling head shews the first liquor to have been taken right.

The 18th century turn of phrase is too delightful not to share with the modern craft brewer, but for those of you who find Ellis' style too wearisome, here are a few thoughts about his method.

(i)   I suggest we stop after two mashes. It is unlikely that the small-scale brewer can be bothered to make a neighbour wort or a blue wort for use as a mash liquor the following day.

(ii) The first liquor temperature is given as "not scalding". This is much higher than the 1736 London method, which added enough cold water to reduce the liquor "to blood heat". Not scalding would mean in the mid seventies Celsius (167°F).

(iii) Boiling the hops for 90 minutes is also a departure from 1736. In earlier versions of this recipe any boiling of hops for more than 30 minutes was considered detrimental to the beer. By 1750 Ellis seems to have been the only person still to divide his hop amount into three and add each aliquot at half hourly intervals.

(iv) "When in the right temper," means cool enough to pitch the yeast i.e. less than 30°C (86°F).

(v)   "Cleanse into Barrels," simply means rack off leaving the lees behind and any floating objects such as bits of hop.

(vi) There was a feeling abroad in the 18th century that the higher dried a malt was, the lower the mash temperature should be. Combrune produced a table of drying heats, which enabled brewers to estimate the mash heat. A table of heats, according to Hayes is included in appendix 2.

Also in the 1750 edition of *London & Country Brewer* we find another reference to Porter. In the section entitled, "To make Porter or give a butt of beer a fine tang," there is a recipe, which uses pale malt.

He continues: "This of late has been improved two ways;

"First by mixing two bushels of Pale Malt with six of Brown, which will preserve Butt Beer in a mellow Condition, and cause it to have a pleasant and sweet farewell on the Tongue: and secondly, to further improve and render it more palatable they boil it two hours and a half and work it two days as cold as possible in the Ton; at last they stir it and put a good handful of common salt into the quantity of a But: then, when the yeast has had one rising more they ton it."

RECIPE 5. HISTORICAL.

TO MAKE PORTER OR GIVE BUTT-BEER A FINE TANG. (LONDON & COUNTRY BREWER 1750. PP 276).

Improved Porter.

This brew takes $^1/_3$ pale malt and $^2/_3$ brown. I have taken Ellis' original text from recipe 4 and rendered it shorter and in modern terminology. Otherwise the method is nearly the same.

This recipe may be the watershed point at which the original all-brown-malt Porter attributed to Harwood lost ground to the more sensible pale and brown malt mixture.

Original Gravity	Not known			
London River or well Water	25 litres	23 litres	5 UK gals	5 US gals
Brown malt Pale malt	10.6 kg 3.5 kg	9.8 kg 3.3 kg	23.4 lb 7.8 lb	19 lb 6.3 lb
Copper hops	Goldings Maximum 5% alpha-acid.			
	200g	180g	6.7 oz	5.4 oz

Brewing method:

Mashing

- Bring the mash liquor to the boil and then dilute it with enough cold water to bring it to 75°C (167°F).
- Run the liquor up through the false mash-tun bottom and mash for 30 minutes.
- Prepare a new charge of liquor and run this onto the goods and mash half an hour longer.
- Cover the goods with a layer of malt and let it stand two hours.
- Set the tap and slowly run the wort into the underback.
- Prepare a second mash liquor. When the first wort has been run off, mash a second time with the new charge.

Boiling

- Boil the first and second worts for 2 ½ hours with all the hops.

Fermenting

- Ferment as coolly as possible without stopping the yeast from working. This should take around 2 days.

Racking

- Add a pinch of salt before racking.

Comments
- Adding salt seems to have caused the yeast to rise one more time. This may be because the salt increased the gravity of the wort. However we are told to add a good handful of salt to 44 gallons of Porter. Scaling this down to 5 gallons requires us to take $^1/_9$ of a handful. I hardly think that such a tiny amount of salt would cause sufficient increase in density to cause the yeast to rise. Murphy's water treatment, available from Brupaks of Huddersfield, also suggests adding salt to Porter mash liquor. Unfortunately no explanation is currently available.
- Despite the long boil indicated here Ellis admonishes us thus. "But I am sure that the common brewer is wrong, who boils his hops above thirty minutes; for, by how much longer he boils them, so much more is the beer made worse."

This brew seems to indicate that Butt-Beers (or Porters) made from all brown malt were losing favour the whole time.

In Ellis we also find reference to a technique, which has come to be known as "dry hopping". There may be earlier references but I haven't come across them. This is used nowadays to give a beer a good aroma feel on the tongue, but was originally done to maximise the keeping properties hops lent to a beer. Ellis describes it thus:

"To fine a drink and preserve it in the but. (*London & Country Brewer. 1750. P. 303*)

"If you could secure a But of Beer from staling too soon, and give it a fine Flavour and Body, take a very small meshed Net, and put into it such a quantity of new Hops, as you think proper; in this put in likewise a Stone to sink it to the bottom of the Cask, and at six months' End tap it. But if you would tap a But of Beer quickly, and secure a Drink sound to the last then put a Parcel of used Hops into it, or without a Net, in the Vessel; that is such Hops as have been only boiled a little while in the first Wort."

1.8 SPARGING

Nowadays the wort is removed from the spent grain by sparging which derives from the Old French word *espargier – to sprinkle*. Although the Oxford Dictionary gives the first recorded use as 1560 and its first brewing use as 1839 the word presumably came to England with the Norman Conquerors in 1066. The 1839 date is entirely commensurate with the scholarly work by Roberts of Edinburgh on his treatise on Pale Ale Brewing, (*The Scottish Ale Brewer* 1838). Roberts was a brilliant brewer and scientist with a natural feel for that which was relevant to the science of the brewing process. He may have spoken French and coined the word sparge from *espargier* but is more likely to have had a good knowledge of Latin and derived from *spargere*. However, I'm about to attempt to wrest this brilliant piece of brewing technology from the Scots and give it back to the English.

Sparging is the process by which the sweet wort extract is washed from the goods after mashing. It is very effective and makes use of the fact that many small washes extract better than one large one, hence the rinse cycle in modern washing machines. Roberts set the tap (ran off the first wort) and at the same time sprayed fine jets of water at the surface of the goods from rotating arms. In an ideal world, the run off from the tap was balanced by the liquor input onto the surface of the grain. The question is, how fine does the input have to be to qualify as a sprinkle? When is a spray a spray? *The London & Country Brewer* of 1736, a full 103 years before Roberts' report, tells us that there was a particular way of washing the goods.

"then let all but half a bushel of the malt run very leisurely into it, stirring it all the while with an oar or paddle, that it may not Ball, and when the Malt is all but just mixed with the Water it is enough, which I am sensible is different from the old way and the general present Practice; – for by not stirring or mashing the malt into a Pudding Consistence or thin Mash, the body of it lies in a more loose Condition, that will easier and sooner admit of a quicker and more true passage of the after-ladings of the several Bowls or Jets of hot water, which must run through it before the Brewing is ended."

And later:

"then hot Boiling water must be laded over so slow that one Bowl must run almost off before another is put over, which will occasion the whole Brewing to last about sixteen Hours, especially if the Oundle way is followed, of spending out of the Tap as small as Straw."

I think we have our first recorded sparge, well established in Hertfordshire by 1736. Sixteen hours for a mash and extraction sounds to me as though fine enough jets were used to qualify as the first sparge.

The response elicited from one famous London based Scottish craft brewer when I proposed sparging as an English invention was quite charming and full of Scottish nationalist fervour. His scorn at my suggestion was such that at times his handwriting becomes difficult to decipher. Here is my best effort to put this argument into the public domain. I quote the Scottish side of it.

"Roberts published his book *The Scottish Ale-Brewer and Practical Maltster*, 3 editions 1837, 1846, & 1847. In first and subsequent editions he noted that *sparging* was a Scottish practice but in England, multiple mashes were the norm. He provides drawings of a sparging machine and explanations as to its use. No *inventor* is named, nor patent claimed, although he notes that the machine is available from a Leith coppersmith at a cost of 4 to 6 guineas! A machine that does the job is technology – pissing *as small as straw* for 16 hours is not!!"

Does not every machine have a prototype, used for evaluating the effectiveness of the idea? Surely, it is the idea put into successful practice that is the invention, not the machine which finally goes for sale. Of course no patent was applied for. The method was already in use, in the public domain as we would now say, and had been for 100 years. Wouldn't a patent application would have failed due to lack of original invention?

This is a point of historical importance, certainly to me and I welcome a vigorous discussion from both sides of the Border.

1.9 STRONG BROWN BEER, CALLED STITCH, COMMON BROWN ALE AND STARTING BUTT-BEER

The above methods require a careful balance of liquor running onto the goods and wort being let out the tap. This was an essential feature of 18th and 19th century brewing when it was common to use third or even fourth runnings from the malt to make weaker beers or for use as the mash liquor for a future brew. It all involved keeping the used malt moist several hours, if not a full day and as such the goods were in danger of becoming infected and imparting a sour flavour to the future brews. Thus the goods were kept wet with hot sparge liquor or second mash liquor to prevent bacterial attack. Our much smaller brews require shorter sparging times and I doubt we bother with return worts etc. so we can be more casual about this point.

Durden Park Beer Circle report no qualitative difference between sparging and multiple mashing. This surprises me. Multiple mashes disturb the bed of grist through which the wort and sparge water run and this allows farinaceous material to run through with the washings. Having once achieved a good filter bed, it seems folly to disturb it.

There is no written evidence on gravities of these early Stout Beers but I would make the recipes using entirely brown malt roasted at around 100°C (212°F) for 5 hours to come out the mash tun with a starting gravity of at least 1065. Assuming the brown malt provides a reasonable amount of extract, 1065 may be far too low. Again the Scots come to my assistance. James Mc Crorie points out that 1065 is definitely too low for a *Stout Ale*. He writes "Roberts, in his analysis of 52 Scottish Ales, undertaken in 1837, the weakest, a 32/- Ale had an OG of 1040, 60/- Ale had an OG 1073-1080 and 140/- Ale over 1120!! Remember Porter was weaker than previously available Ales. Generally above 1050 were *Ales*. Less than that were *Beers* (This definition changed throughout history and from one location to another).

Modern brown malts deliver a considerably larger quantity of extract that the Victorian counterparts. The table in appendix 9 compares the extract from Fawcetts' (Castleford) pale and burnt malts. The difference is around 8% which is certainly less than the 20% quoted by *The Brewer 1863*. "This fictitious malt (Blown) was, on the introduction of the Saccharometer found to yield a deficient produce, as compared with Pale, of from 18 to 25 per cent., and the best Brown of from 15 to 20 per cent."

Either Fawcetts are over optimistic, have a different method of comparing extract from malt, or modern brown malts are but a pale imitation of those from early Victorian malts. Care is needed in jumping to the latter conclusion! A blown malt will provide much less material per bushel than a normal malt.

Stitch was simply a weaker Stout and as such referred to as Strong Brown Beer. A strong Stout was made (1075) and run on with more sparge water. I would stop the tap at 1065 and boil with more hops.

Stitch was thought to possess medicinal properties, although there is nothing in it to set it apart from other dark beers, apart from more or less alcohol. However, Ellis recalls that one Mr. Medicott esq. used Stitch "at the beginning of a Consumption, and I heard him say, it did him very great service, for he lived many years afterwards".

Even today I observe that a single cure by a medicine, is enough to provide that medicine with some magical scientific property, which no one doubts. Little wonder then that in the 18th century people grasped at straws when confronted by an invariably terminal illness such as tuberculosis.

Common Brown Ale and Starting Beer were sparged even more than Stitch. After the stiff and second mash the goods were capped with fresh malt. The original text becomes very confused at this point but I believe it to mean that after resting and setting the tap, this third wort was boiled one hour with a few hops, possibly spent from a stronger brew. The text actually says that *the goods* were boiled one hour! Our initial response is to cry "misprint". One says nowadays that the practice of sparging too hot or too long extracts tannins from the malt and imparts an unpleasant side flavour. Perhaps this tannin flavour was regarded as acceptable or even desirable. I actually think the case is over stated. Continental decoction mashes cause the thin mash liquor, containing a fair amount of malt, to be brought to the boil several times. Hornsey (*Brewing* 1999) in his excellent book on modern brewing chemistry doesn't mention tannins but merely says that over sparging by using liquor which is too hot, causes phenols and dextrins to be extracted which are undesirable in sweet wort.

Some of the Victorian Stouts and Porters described by Amsinck have very complicated sparge and multi mash techniques. Bickersdyke surmises that this leached out these taste components, and these were seen as an essential part of the "Porter" taste.

However, we will never sparge to the extent that profit orientated breweries currently do or Victorian breweries did. In fact tannins are not a group of compounds with a defined structure. They have an astringent taste. Many are glycosides and dealt with easily by amylase and converted to a glucose; others are esters and likely to be hydrolysed during a prolonged acidic boil. Let's forget about them as a problem! Boil the goods if you have a mind to but make the mash thin! Maybe the taste is authentic.

To find out what this is all about, see page 174

RECIPE 6. HISTORICAL.

STITCH (LONDON & COUNTRY 1736 SECTION 42).

Stitch or Strong Brown Ale.				
Stitch is made in the same way as a London Stout but the runnings are greater in volume and it has a considerably higher hopping rate.				
Original Gravity	Not known – Aim at 1065			
Hard well water	25 litres	23 litres	5 UK gals	5 US gals
Brown malt	17 kg	15.7 kg	37 lb	30 lb
Copper hops	Goldings Maximum 5% alpha-acid.			
	88g	80g	3 oz	2.4 oz

Brewing method:
First stiff mash.
- Bring the first liquor nearly to the boil with a good covering of malt husks to accelerate the process.
- Ladle both the liquor and husks into the mash tun and allow to cool until you can see your face clearly in the liquor.
- Run the malt in slowly, keeping a pound back. Stir during the addition to prevent balling occurring.
- This should be a genuinely stiff mash.
- Use the remaining malt to cover the goods.
- Rest the mash 2 to 3 hours.

Second mash.
- Set a new liquor charge heating, this time to boiling point.
- Set the tap and run off a small amount of wort and replace it with near boiling water from the boiler.
- This process was repeated until the correct quantity of wort was achieved for a particular beer or the copper was full.
- A second mash was used in addition to the washing if a thinner beer was required.

Boiling
- Put 30g (1oz) hops in a muslin bag. (Canvas was the 18th century choice) and boil in the wort for 30 minutes. Replace the hops with a second aliquot and boil for another 30 minutes. Repeat this one more time so a total boil of 90 minutes is achieved. For a keeping beer it seems the spent hops may not have been removed before the next addition.

Fermentation
- Ferment out in the way described in recipe 2. Keep several weeks before serving.

Alcohol Content	Unknown
Bitterness: 9 EBU	
Colour: Dark brown	

Comments
- If no small beer was made from a previous mash then the second running was used as the first liquor for the next brew.
- The hop amounts are guesswork for a Stitch beer and are based on what was common for a small brewer doing a moderately strong March Ale.

RECIPE 7. HISTORICAL.

STARTING BUTT-BEER (LONDON & COUNTRY 1736 SECTION 42).

Butt Beer. Starting Butt-Beer was fermented cooler than Stout, a shorter length drawn than for Common Brown Ale but boiled 90 minutes with more hops. That apart it was made in the same way as London Stout but the runnings were greater in volume and it has a considerably higher hopping rate.				
Original Gravity	Not known – Aim at 1055			
Hard well water	25 litres	23 litres	5 UK gals	5 US gals
Brown malt	15.8 kg	14.5 kg	34 lb	28 lb
Copper hops	Goldings Maximum 5% alpha-acid.			
	60g	50g	2 oz	1.75 oz

RECIPE 8. HISTORICAL.

COMMON BROWN BEER (LONDON & COUNTRY 1736 SECTION 42).

Common Brown Ale. Common Brown Beer is made in the same way as Stitch but the runnings are greater in volume and it has a slightly lower hopping rate.				
Original Gravity	Not known – Aim at 1050			
Hard well water	25 litres	23 litres	5 UK gals	5 US gals
Brown malt	14.2 kg	13 kg	31 lb	25 lb
Copper hops	Goldings Maximum 5% alpha-acid.			
	56g	50g	2 oz	1.75 oz

RECIPE 9. HISTORICAL.

BROWN ALE (LONDON & COUNTRY 1736 SECTION 42).

October Brown Ale.
Another set of parameters for brown ale is also given. Again use the general method for London Stout but the runnings are greater in volume and it has a considerably higher hopping rate.

Original Gravity	Not known – Aim at 1075			
Hard well water	25 litres	23 litres	5 UK gals	5 US gals
Brown malt	21.7 kg	20 kg	48 lb	39 lb
Copper hops	Goldings Maximum 5% alpha-acid.			
	132g	122g	4.4 oz	3.6 oz

The *London & Country Brewer* excuses the random attitude to hop amounts in these recipes with the sentence, "The allowance of Hops for Ale or Beer, cannot be exactly adjusted without coming to particulars, because the Proportion should be according to the nature and quality of the Malt, the Season of the Year it is brew'd in, and the length of time it is to be kept." He doesn't even try to come to terms with annual variations in hop quality. Pale ales were definitely hopped at anything up to twice the rate for Brown Beers, but the latter varies from next to nothing to quite appreciable rates. You choose!

The rule seems to be that the longer a wort is run then the more hops are needed. Presumably the bitter burnt taste of the brown malt diminishes and so it was worth investing a reasonable amount of hops in the gyle.

We are indebted to the Durden Park Beer Circle for their research into brewing a 1750s Porter using only modern ingredients. This is what they came up with.

RECIPE 10. HISTORICAL.

FROM RESEARCH BY DR. J. HARRISON IN THE WHITBREAD BREWING ARCHIVE.

Durden Original Porter (1750).

The Circle writes of this recipe: "1750 Porters would have contained mostly brown malt. These cannot be made satisfactorily from present day-brown malts. The above recipe is constructed to meet contemporary descriptions of 1750 Porter, i.e. black, strong, bitter and nutritious. It is one of he Circle's favourite old beers."

My thanks go to members of the Durden Park Beer Circle in West London for allowing me to use their work.

Original Gravity	1090		22.5° Plato	
No analysis.	25 litres	23 litres	5 UK gallons	5 US gallons
Pale Malt	8.95 kg	8.23 kg	17.5 lbs	14.2 lbs
Brown Malt	1.28 kg	1.18 kg	2.5 lbs	2 lbs
Crystal Malt	1.28 kg	1.18 kg	2.5 lbs	2 lbs
Black Malt	640g	590g	1.3 lbs	1 lbs
Copper & Dry	Fuggles 4 – 5% alpha–acid.			
Copper	45g	40g	1.5 oz	1.2 oz
Dry hops	3g	3g	0.1 oz	0.1 oz

Brewing method:
- Add hot water to the ground grain to produce a very stiff mash at 66°C (150°F)
- Maintain this temperature for 180 minutes.
- Raise the temperature to 77°C (170°F) for 30 minutes.
- Sparge very slowly with water at 82–85°C (182–185°F) until the wort running off is of gravity 1075 (19°P)
- Change the vessel receiving the wort and continue sparging down to 1040 (10°P)
- Boil the second weaker wort until the gravity is 1075 (19°P).
- Mix the worts and boil with the hops for another 90 minutes
- Cool, strain and rinse the hops.
- Adjust to the required gravity by adding cold boiled water or dried pale malt extract as needed.
- Ferment with a good quality ale yeast.
- Dry hop with $\frac{1}{10}$ oz (3g) Goldings.
- Mature for 4 months.

Comments:
- Durden Park members have contrived to give us a look-alike 1750s Porter only using off the peg ingredients readily available through a reasonable retailer.
- The alternative is to look at Combrune's table of drying heats for 18th century brown malts and try to darken some malt accordingly.
- Appendix 1 of Old British Beers And How To Make Them has some suggestions for converting modern readily available malt types into substitutes for yesteryear beers. A summary of their work is included in appendix 5.
- The Historical Companion to House-Brewing has instructions for making green malt, which can be converted into the real thing (maybe).

1.10 HERTFORDSHIRE METHOD OF MASHING AND EXTRACTING

This method of brewing strong or October Beer seems to have been common "throughout Hertfordshire and other remote parts of the Country". It was probably used for Stout beers, which were generally brewed as strong as any when considering bushels of malt per barrel of Stout.

"There was a man in this Country that brewed for a Gentleman constantly after a very precise method, and that was, as soon as he had put over all his first copper of water and mashed it some time, he would directly let the Cock run a small stream and presently put some fresh malt on the former and mash all the while the Cock was spending, which he would put again over the Malt, as often as his Pail or Hand-bowl was full, and this for an hour or two together. Then he would let it run off intirely, and put it over at once, to run off again as small as a Straw."

I had thought the modern day RIMS method had found its first exponent with the German brewer Hahn, whose brewing machine now forms the logo for the Craft Brewers' Association, but it seems those Hertfordshire men beat him by some 70 years.

1750 – 1800

2.1 PORTER AND THE NAVY

We have seen that Porter brewing in the first half of the 18th century was condemned to succeed. The economic advantages of brewing a strong dark beer were enormous. It utilised the darker more forgiving malts, required less and lower quality hops and was a popular replacement to the mixtures, which the drinking public demanded. Porter also lent itself to the brewing water common in London, which meant that as the metropolis expanded, London brewers had a ready market, with only limited transport problems. London water is not ideal brewing water and dark beers, which would never achieve a high degree of brightness, covered a multitude of brewing sins.

On top of that, in the days before gravity measurements were easy or common, darkness was equated with strength, at least in the mind of the drinker. And although we may scoff at this notion it is of course, tinged with an element of truth. If we brew a pale beer with only English pale malt, Marris Otter or Pipkin, the malt, although pale, does impart colour. Therefore, if our craft brewer produces a gyle with 9kg (19 lbs) malt per 48 litres (9 gallons) he may expect a wort gravity around 1055. If he brews again but this time makes only 6 gallons of pale ale the gravity may well be 1075 but the colour will darken from straw to amber. Even the non-discerning drinker will spot the quality and colour change between 1055 and 1075 OG in a pale ale. It was thus fairly easy to convince drinkers that the addition of dark malt was a "good" thing. It was a short step to move from two ales of similar strength but different colour, to one ale being perceived as stronger than the other, just because of its colour. It's called marketing. The problem is we think we invented it!

But there was another factor, which made Porter the beer of the century. As communications improved with the advent of canals and the beginning of road building as we know it, it became economically viable to ship beer beyond the end of the street. In an effort to win markets and meet demand, breweries needed to become bigger. There were two limitations though; the size vessel a cooper could deliver for mashing, storing etc. and how to ferment in summer. The former was an engineering problem and with new materials and techniques becoming rapidly available, it was a problem with a solution. Fermenting in summer was much more intractable. The fermentation slows as the fermentable sugar is used up. The yeast uses the sugars as an energy supply and so this slow-down is coupled with a reduction in carbon dioxide production. Experienced brewers need hardly use a hydrometer to follow the progress of a fermentation. They simply monitor by eye the rate of carbon dioxide production. However, it is the bubbles of this gas sweeping through the fermentation that keeps the yeast cells distributed in homogenous wort. Furthermore the high starting gravity of a wort helps the cells swim or remain suspended within the liquid. As the sugars are used up by the yeast, the density of the wort decreases and without enough gas being evolved to mix the wort, the yeast cells tend to settle out. This actually occurs long before the racking gravity has been achieved and without enough yeast cells colliding with sugar molecules there is a real danger of the fermentation sticking. This was a fairly easy problem to tackle when brewing was being done on a relatively small scale. The beer was regularly roused (stirred) towards the end of a fermentation.

Unfortunately for the brewer a fermentation isn't a simple single reaction or process. There are two identifiable types of fermentation and innumerable reactions taking place within them. During the first hours (so called lag phase) not much carbon dioxide production is evident. The yeast is using up all the available oxygen dissolved in the wort for aerobic reproduction. This uses up sugar, makes carbon dioxide but not so much alcohol but produces new young yeast cells. As the yeast cell concentration goes up, the gas production becomes evident and the fermentation takes hold proper.

Many microbes, but especially the fungi, have the ability to switch from aerobic to anaerobic respiration, should the oxygen supply begin to dwindle. This is what happens when the yeast cell concentration reaches a high enough level and eventually all the dissolved oxygen is used up. Anaerobic sugar conversion produces much less heat, hardly any carbon dioxide but more alcohol. But with the onset of anaerobic fermentation came the time the old brewer had to rouse, which inevitably introduced oxygen and increased the rate of the highly exothermic aerobic reproduction reaction.

As fermentation vats increased in size so the surface area to volume ratio began to favour heat retention within the vat. This is because if we assume a cylindrical vat shape, the surface area, through which heat can be lost to the environment goes up as a square of the increasing radius, whilst the volume increases as the radius cubed. Everything mitigated to increasing heat retention, which speeds up the rate of reaction by causing more yeast/sugar collisions. So as the vats became bigger the problem of hot wild fermentations ceased to be one encountered only in high summer but became a problem throughout the year. The Victorians used the new fridge technology and fitted attemperators to their fermentation vats, which then put another nail in the dark-beer coffin, but we are not that far yet. In the 18th century even the developing transport system mitigated in favour of Brown Beer brewing. There were ever more reasons to brew darker beers. They solved the problems. Using brown malt meant less fermentable material and was thus a waste of money, but it also reduced the chances of a yeast cell colliding with a sugar molecule.

The reaction rate went down, less heat per minute was produced and the fermentation remained cool. The wort didn't blast its way out the vat, propelled by excessive carbon dioxide production and end up running down the gutter outside in the street.

We also know that hot fermentations cause side tastes and general drop in quality of all types of beer. The Admiralty would commission brews at any time of the year, but especially in summer when they were most active and sailors often had to complain of "foxed" beer, a condition common when warm fermentations have been used. Thus it was that London Porter brewers brewed from September through to June, whilst the Burton Pale Ale brewers would start in October and never brew beyond May. Porter left only three months with no brewing activity and by brewing it good and strong with high hopping ratios, enough beer could be brewed in cooler parts of the year to last through the high demand summer months.

Porter brewing also had another unforeseen advantage. It seems that its black burnt flavour was more forgiving of warm fermentations and foxed beer. If you had to have unavoidable side tastes then Porter masked them best.

Protz (*Classic Stout & Porter* 1997) reports the use of attemperation as early as 1760, done by pumping cold water, delivered with copper pipes, through the *"maturing"* beer. Again he keeps his source secret. It is difficult to understand why the beer would need cooling during maturation, when London cellars settle at around 12-16°C (45-54°F). We know that wort cooling still had to be done in large open vessels some the size of a swimming pool situated on the brewery roof. In warm weather it took a day to cool and so there was no shortage of dust and other solid matter to settle out from the wort. According to A.C. Reavenall, Head brewer at Charrington's in 1957, the introduction of plate coolers in the Charrington's Brewery did not occur until 1890 but fermentations were attemperated much earlier.

Throughout the 16th and 17th centuries the Spanish, Portuguese, Dutch and English merchants had been pushing further afield. Journeys to the East Indies in search of spices stretched the resources in ship-building and the strength of the crew way beyond the technology of the time. Thus it was that ships were often worn out before they had completed the outward journey and it was common to overman a ship in the hope that enough sailors would survive to bring it safely home. Even with double manning ships often had to be abandoned due to lack of fit manpower. The wisdom that citrus fruits would prevent scurvy had been learnt in the early 17th century. Milton (*Nathaniel's Nutmeg* 1999) points out that in 1601 the *Red Dragon* sailed for the East Indies with cider for 8 months at 1 quart per day per man and beer for 4 months at 1 bottle per day per man. The captain put ashore wherever he thought he would find fresh lemons and he took the juice of lemons with him for the next stage of the voyage. This knowledge seems to have been lost again, although Captain Cook knew that the ill health of the crew was a dietary problem. Nevertheless, it took many years before it became common to try to remediate the vitamin C deficiency with fruit and vegetables. Sailors did continue to take beer to sea, and they brewed themselves too by taking concentrated wort, diluting it and fermenting and then immediately drinking the beverage. Thus it was that their vitamin B levels were maintained. There is sound evidence that the first extract home brewers were sailors. Captain Cook's logs abound with references to "inspissated wort". For a while I feared that the Aussies were not only tonking us Poms at cricket, rugby and anything else to do with balls, but would also claim the first instance of home brewing on one of Cook's voyages of discovery. In fact one Mr. Pelham did much research on land into thickening or inspissating worts (from the Latin *spissus*) and started brewing from hopped wort extracts off the coast of Africa, on the New Zealand voyage of 1772 in the *Resolution*. According to *Selections from his Journals 1768-1779* he took 80 bushels of malt and 19 half barrels of the "Inspissated Juice of Beer." The good news is he didn't home brew in Australia so home brew seems to remain a British contribution. Clerke brewed on board too, but said sailors were reluctant to drink his brew, which he put down to fickleness, not lack of quality.

Cook was not an academic man by nature but he did write a famous tract for the Admiralty on prevention of scurvy. One Admiral J. Dalrymple went further. So impressed was he about the value of beer as a prophylactic against scurvy that he tried to do the 18th century equivalent of patent a malt loaf, from which one could extract wort as and when required. Unfortunately he doesn't include a huge amount of detail, the reason being no doubt, that in the absence of patent law he didn't want someone else stealing his idea. His tract written for the Admiralty in 1795 and called *Supplying fresh made beer at sea* comes as close as one can without losing masculine street cred to pleading with the Admiralty to address the scurvy problem effectively by using beer. It wasn't fashionable to feel sorry for servants and deck hands but economic necessity and the appalling losses suffered by the newly formed East India Company made them begin to consider the effect that sailor health was having on profits.

Dalrymple suggested 1 quarter malt : 1 cwt molasses, or ½ cwt raw sugar. He made a cold infusion of hops to "draw all watery, oily and impure parts from both and therby form them into a cake of both." A slurry was made from sugar and malt, mixed with hop infusion and pressed and dried to form a cake. This kept during a voyage presumably due to the high sugar content preventing bacterial growth. Putrid water was often all that was available and so he checked his method worked with any water (except sea water) but did point out that the nature of the water did impact on the quality of the beer. Nevertheless, brewing with the water reduced the effects of putrefaction. He seems to have known that bacterial concentrations in the wort were reduced by working with a strong yeast but of course didn't use that terminology. He didn't know what a microbe was so we have to touch our forelocks in deference to his perceptiveness!

No hop amounts were given. When required he put the cake and yeast into water and within 2 days a brisk fermentation had begun, which is hardly surprising in tropical heat. To prevent spoilage the sea-men drank the beverage as soon as fermentation began to abate and only enough for 3 days was brewed. His method had to rely on the ability of someone to brew every three days and that person couldn't be the cook as he had enough to do. Furthermore all thickening and manufacture of the cake was done on land as it was quite impossible to commandeer the galley for heating large volumes of liquid. No details are given on the nature of the yeast, apart from the fact it was dried.

More noble beers had hop extract added along with the water. Porter, which was most tolerant of this rude treatment had the hop fla-vour dried into the cake.

Homebrew at sea was always fraught with problems and done as a last resort. The picture below shows the *Grand Turk,* a recreated frig-ate from the time of the Napoleonic wars. This ship was used in the Hornblower TV series. It is tiny; around 30m and 10m at its maximum length and breadth! Imagine it being over-manned and then one should homebrew for the whole crew every three days. The Endeavour was 40 years earlier and smaller still.

The Endeavour and Grand Turk are recreated sailing ships, direct copies of their Porter heyday ancestors. The sailors brewed on board such vessels.

RECIPE 11. HISTORICAL.

ADMIRAL DALRYMPLE'S PORTER. 1795.

Seaman's Porter

This was brewed as strong as a "Strong Beer" which was at least 1080 in the 18th century.

Sickness on board ship cost many lives and the fighting efficiency of the navy was correspondingly reduced. As early as 1775 Captain Cook was brewing on board and on a three year voyage lost only one man, but carrying the utensils and wort had always been problematic. The utensils were cumbersome and the worts likely to go off. Board brewing was nevertheless easier than trying to transport large amounts of beer.

Admiral Dalrymple urged the Navy to carry the ingredients as dried cakes and dried yeast. He is very cagey about exactly how this was to be done but then plagiarism was rife. I suggest the following method.

Original Gravity	1080		20° Plato	
Anything available	25 litres	23 litres	5 UK gals	5 US gals
Pale Malt Brown malt Sugar	7.1 kg 1.0 kg ½ cwt	6.5 kg 0.8kg	15.6 lbs 2 lbs	12.6 lbs 1.8 lbs
Infusion	Goldings 5% alpha-acid. Make an infusion by boiling 20 minutes in 15 litres (3 gallons) water			
	253g	232g	8.3 oz	6.7 oz

Brewing method:
- Add hot water hop infusion to a mixture to the ground grain and sugar to produce a stiff mash at 66°C (150°F)
- Maintain this temperature for 180 minutes.
- Warm the goods and evaporate the liquid to leave a cake.
- Allow to cool.
- When the beer is required mix the cake with water containing the yeast powder.
- Ferment right out, keg and begin to serve immediately

Comments:
- In fact Dalrymple was left to a much more haphazard brewing method. Firstly he assumed it would be impossible to prevail upon the cook to let him heat his hot water for the hop infusion so cold water at hold temperature was added. This varied between 13°C (56°F) in Scotland in winter to 29°C (84°F), which he described as the common heat in Jamaica.
- He also had to contend with putrid water, which he claims was greatly improved after being used to wash out the malt/sugar cake. In his experiment he took loch water, three months old and contaminated with the "shambles, tan-works and common sewers of the city. I put no warm water to it, but worked in a common fire room. In a few hours it began to ferment. From that time the putrid taste and smell became less and less until they entirely ceased and the beer was made in two days or more."
- Drinking beer so young brought with it its own problems too. "But if any of the seamen should find the briskness of the beer was attended with flatulencies, this might be prevented by mixing with it a part of their allowances of spirits."

On land we are left with much less information on Porter drinking. As indicated, unlike claret it hardly ever found its way into the literature of the time. Jane Austen's work has been carefully analysed by Maggie Lane (*Jane Austen and Food* 1995) in order to get some idea what was taken in the way of food and drink. Even when meals are described we are not told what was drunk but on one occasion. Willoughby's quick lunch in the coaching inn in Marlborough (*Sense and Sensibility*) is only described because he wants to deny Elinor's imputation that he is drunk. He ate muscles and washed it down with Porter.

So if no one talked of Porter, where did it all go? Mathias (*The Brewing Industry in England 1700-1830* 1959) has calculated that by the end of 18th century London Porter brewers were achieving 83 000 barrels per year but by 1830 this had risen to 250 000 barrels, almost all from London. Prolific stuff! If huge quantities were being consumed in town and country and yet no mention is made of its importance I can only assume it was so common as to be self evident that Porter was the drink in all everyday circumstances, rather like tea or coffee today.

This assumption is substantiated by a description of a Royal Society dinner in 1784. The French botanist Monsieur Faujas de Saint Fond was a guest and recorded, "The beefsteaks and the roast beef were at first drenched with copious quantities of strong beer, called Porter, drunk out of cylindrical pewter pots, which are much preferred to glasses because one can swallow a whole pint at a draught." This description is unclear. Did they pour the Porter over the beef or was his use of "drenched" referring to how much Porter they drank with the beef?

The philosophers at the dinner went on to port, Madeira and claret, which were used to drink the health of the Prince of Wales and all present, one by one for it would be impolite to do a bulk toast. Some Champagne followed by tea, then brandy and rum and other strong liqueurs. The whole banquet was such a hoot that I include Faujas' complete description in appendix 7 but the key is that we have to rely on a Frenchman's description? It doesn't seem that it was remarkable enough to attract the attention of an English writer.

2.2 THE LUNATIC FRINGE AND JUST PLAIN QUAINT

The other main feature of Porter brewing towards the end of the 18th century was adulteration. This was often done with the very best of intentions as in the case of Childs (*Everyman his Brewer 1790*), who urged the working family to brew at home to save money and enjoy a nutritional beverage. It would not be fair to say that the effects of these adulterations were not known but it was considered acceptable to allow the brewing market to regulate itself. This meant that those who didn't want the benefit of seriously narcotic substances would drink in a pub that made good clean nutritional Porter. Unfortunately in the absence of regulation the use of adulterants gained the upper hand, was welcomed by the drinker and eventually had to be banned. This in turn led to a home-brew subculture that wasn't governed by the law of 1816 demanding only malt, hops, water and yeast should go into beer. This law it seems was only applied to commercial breweries and home brewers were urged to continue the practice of adding adulterants to beer. Eventually it was suppressed by banning the sale of the narcotic substances. Here is one of the worst home brew recipes of the 1790s borrowed in this form from *The Historical Companion to House Brewing (2nd edition 2003)*.

Interestingly Childs quotes the following from Combrune's Theory of Brewing on the title page of *Every Man his own Brewer – A Practical Treatise, Explaining The Art And Mystery Of Brewing Porter.*

"Some COOPERS attempt to extend their art so far as to add strength to the BEER; but let it be remembered, that the principle constituent parts of Beer SHOULD BE MALT and HOPS; when strength is given to the liquor by any other means, its nature is altered, and it is no more Beer that we drink."

He seems to have forgotten this wisdom by the time he wrote page 8 of *Everyman his own Brewer*. He advises everything but the kitchen sink.

RECIPE 12. HISTORICAL.
PORTER (CHILDS 1798).

Quack's Porter
I don't believe this was in any way a true Porter but a look-a-like. Various colouring agents such as burnt sugar and liquorice replaced the traditional brown malt. Nevertheless, these adulterated brews went under the name of Porter for many decades and cannot really be ignored. Thirty years later Tuck had the following to say of this home brew and its larger brewery cousin. "This farrago of filth! Every age will produce its quacks but that such excessive ignorance could so impose upon the public to cause this pamphlet to pass through eleven editions is astonishing". Oddly enough Tuck went on to quote the entire recipes for the homebrew and brewery versions, so much did he despise them.

Original Gravity	Not given.			
Water not specified	25 litres	23 litres	5 UK gals	5 US gals
Malt: Amber	4.3 kg	3.9 kg	8.6 lb.	7 lb.
Copper hops	Probably something like Fuggles, alpha acid 5%.			
	130 g	120 g	4 oz	3.3 oz
Treacle	270 g	250 g	8 oz	6.4 oz
Spanish Liquorice	130 g	120 g	4 oz	3.2 oz
Essentia bina	130 g	120 g	4 oz	3.2 oz
Colour	130 g	120 g	4 oz	3.2 oz
Capsicum/ginger	pinch	pinch	pinch	pinch

Brewing method.
- Prepare the mash tun by laying a clean wisp of hay or straw at the bottom to prevent the malt running off with the liquor.
- Empty the malt in the mash tun and bring the liquor to the boil.
- Dash the liquor with cold water until it smartly bites the finger. If you have a thermometer, this will be 82°C (180°F). The second wort will be run on at 88°C (190°F).
- Ladle the water over the malt until properly wetted.
- Prepare the ingredients and add them to the first wort.
This was probably mashed and infused at around 66°C (150°F) for 1 hour.
- Put a few hops in the receiving back in summer to prevent the wort souring.
- Boil the first wort with the ingredients.
- Pitch the yeast and ferment out.
- Ready to drink after 1 week

Comments:
- These original amounts made 6 gallons of Porter from 1 peck of malt i.e. 2 gallons. Only people in lodgings would have made such a short length brew. Many other things were added for the full 5 barrel version, and they are so poisonous that it would not have been safe to add them to such a small gyle. This is what also went into the 5 barrel version.

Cocculus Indicus – ¼ oz. Considered to be less stupefying than cinnamon, but known as a violent poison.

Salt of tartar – 2 drachms. Probably acidic potassium tartrate, available as wine stone after fermenting wine.

Heading – ¼ oz. This was a one to one mixture of aluminium sulphate and copper sulphate and produced and astounding head on the Porter (and the drinkers). Copper sulphate would be banned nowadays in foodstuffs and aluminium sulphate is suspected by some in cases of Alzheimer's disease although there is no hard evidence.

Ginger – 3 oz

Lime – 4 oz. We are not told what sort of lime, probably calcium oxide.

Linseed – 1 oz. A powerful laxative.

Cinnamon – 2 drachms

Childs notes:
- If the strike temperature was too high then the malt set and did not dissolve up in the liquor.
- Always run the wort onto a bed of hops in summer to prevent it turning sour.
- The copper hops were increased by a third in summer.
- Amber malt was preferred to pale or brown.
- Essentia bina was made by boiling sugar in an iron pan (copper was not tough enough) until it was dark brown and bitter. Add a little water to it to prevent it setting hard on cooling.
- Colouring was sugar not treated so rudely as essentia bina, but retaining a yellow colour.

There was no hesitation by Childs in asserting that this is the only way for families to make Porter.

This is how the 1863 edition of *The Brewer* summed up the malaise, which was presumably still prevalent in house breweries. Firstly though he railed against brown or blown malt, which was already feeling the economic pressures.

"This fictitious malt (Blown) was, on the introduction of the Saccharometer found to yield a deficient produce, as compared with Pale, of from 18 to 25 per cent., and the best Brown of from 15 to 20 per cent. These discoveries, combined with the high price of hops in certain seasons, led to the furtive introduction of many illicit substitutes, several of which are in a high degree poisonous, and the employment of which cannot be too strongly condemned. Spanish liquorice root, both in the powder and in the juice, and black resin were used to impart flavour as well as colour. Molasses, raw grain, and sugar, took the place of malt. Gentian, or bitterwort root, marsh trefoil and quassia, all became substitutes for hops, and alum to clarify it. A sensation of warmth was produced by capsicum: sometimes by salt of steel, and sometimes by copperas: though the last two were employed, the former to produce a retentive head, the latter to tinge it brown, by its affinity for oxygen.

Fictitious strength was imparted by the coculus indicus and the bitter bean of St. Ignatius. Tobacco and nux-vomica (rank narcotic poisons) were introduced with the same object."

Our writer mixed the uses of copperas and salt of steel. Iron II salts turn brown by the oxidising effect of air upon them. He goes on to cite the use of honey, saccharine, caraway, and coriander seeds as stimulants, jalap as an effervescent, and corrective of acidity (lactobacilli infection), ginger, grains of Paradise, orange peel; long pepper etc. were boiled in the copper."

If the literature is to be believed such use was so widespread that the history of Porter cannot ignore these additives. That too was Porter!!

Oddly enough it may have been the hydrometer, which caused the increase in adulteration up to 1816. The realisation that brown malt was an expensive way to brew beer led to increasing use of paler malts in Porters. Wheeler's Patent Malt of 1817 allowed even more pale to be used and the Patent Malt provided the colour. Unfortunately for the brewer it didn't taste much like Porter and so adulterations may have been used to redress the flavour problem as brown malt fell from favour.

The 19th Century

3.1 THE RATIONALISATION PROCESS

There was no shortage of interesting mashing techniques as is illustrated by this Porter gyle from *The Complete Brewer or Art & Mystery of Brewing* published in London around 1802. I would have dated it as 1760 at the latest except that the thermometer was rarely available and worts were not commonly being weighed to get ideas about gravity before the turn of the century. Otherwise this shows how little things moved in some areas, while others were storming ahead.

- Equipment – Strong beers or October beers (this would include Porter) were worked in a double water bath vessel with perforated false bottom. There were two taps, one for inner one for outer vessel. This allowed the water to be replaced in the outer vessel and thus maintain the correct heat in the mash tun. Larger gyles don't suffer from heat loss and so these must have been very small indeed. He notes, "Family brewing will not achieve the Porter quality achieved in brew houses", presumably because of problems of heat loss from small gyles during the mash.

- Ingredients – Specifically when brewing Porter we are admonished, "Don't use ox blood but elderberry juice. Elderberry brings the Porter on to the quality of fine old Porter, which gets its quality by being long kept in a larger quantity." Later editions of the *London & Country Brewer* mention the use of elderberry to impart the character of claret. I have always suspected the adulterations were used in order to give Porter a longer lease of life. Maybe economic pressures and the move of the classes with purchasing power towards French wine pushed Porter brewers to try these absurd customs. During the long years of privation caused by the Napoleonic Wars claret was not to be had at any price. Was this an attempt to fill a market gap?

- Malt should be high dried with culm (Welsh anthracite) and only one malt type should be used. "I have already observed, that the real flavour of Porter, as originally drank, is completely lost; and this by pale malts being introduced. As the old practice will hardly be taken up, suffice it to say, our ancestors brewed Porter entirely with high dried malt, while in the present day, in many houses, high dried or blown malts are entirely omitted. I confess, the finest gyle of beer I ever turned out, was from fifty quarters of fine Ware amber, with the first liquor being taken at 160°F. However I advise the young brewer to make a mixture of blown, amber, and pale, in equal quantities, always remembering to grind into his tun the pale first, the amber next and then the brown."

- Of hops we are told that they should be "good strong ripe brown hops, with the seeds in them full and dry."

- Heats – One always believed that pale malts would stand higher heats in the tun. This led to some interesting calculations for mash heats.

E.g.

Pale mashed at	178°F
Amber mashed at	166°F
Brown mashed at	166°F
Sum	510
Averaged	510/3 = 170°F

This assumed equal proportions of malt types. If this were not the case then the larger quantity would have its heat weighted in the averaging calculation.

E.g.

1 quarter pale malt	178°F
2 quarters amber	2 x 166°F
2 quarters brown	2 x 166°F
Sum	842
Averaged	842/5 = 168°F

The Hayes heats are shown for various malts in appendix 3.

- Water – Soft water is best but "(Porter) brewing is not naturally limited to London." 12 pails in the copper wet 5 bushels malt, and make a hogshead of beer wort. This would be around 8kg (18 lb.) of malt for 25 litres. Quite a brew. Water is run into the copper with ¼ lb hops.

- Liquor preparation – (I paraphrase) "When the water begins to be hot sprinkle ½ peck malt on. Don't stir. Let the malt swim until the water begins to simmer. Ladle the water or run it out the copper and put it in the mash tub. This creates a lot of steam".

- Mash temperatures – They knew the value of the correct temperature but how to describe it and achieve it was the challenge. In fact it described by steps such as, "wait until you can see your reflection in the liquor", which actually means, "wait for the steam to clear". This indeed gives a strike temperature of around 75°C (167°F). Our author wrote, " In the common way the malt is put into the water when it is of this fit degree of heat, as well as the brewer can judge it, and in general tolerably right." 1¾ hour mash was usual.

- Malt – Brewers weren't fussed about using slack malt. They didn't have much choice. Nevertheless they cracked the malt and left it to, "mellow some time in air. Brown malt three days, pale one or two."

- Holding the mash temperature – "This may be done by placing the mashing tub in a larger vessel full of hot water, which may be replenished with fresh heated water as it cools." "In this way 2 hours will extract the full virtue of the malt."

- Mashing – "Save a half bushel, the rest is mashed into the liquor, leisurely and slowly while someone else stirs. Do not beat it to break it. All parts should be wet. Beating causes the same effect as grinding too farinaceous." When well stirred in, sprinkle on the half held back to insulate the surface. "When the mash is finished, the liquor impregnated with the strength of the malt is let out the receiver and strained from the grains." No wash! To give it the flavour and virtue of the hop – "rub hops to pieces, place in bag, run hot wort slowly over them. Boil with the hops for a few minutes".

- Sparging – Run in boiling water at the same time as the tap is opened. A stream of water as thick as a crow's quill should be achieved. Run off the first wort over all the hops- put hops and wort in boiler and boil ¼ hour. No more! Collect the liquor in the underback.

- Hopping – This is for the prime wort. Pump it up to copper. Put in a bag of hops or sprinkle them on. Boil until they sink. Long boiling is unnecessary and to the detriment of the beer. Dry old hops sink too soon though.

- Boil – Boiling is finished when a bowl of hot wort curdles and separates on standing to cool. Test the taste. A quick boil helps the break. Old malt breaks sooner. Long boils spoil the light pleasant flavour of the hop. "Brew each, strong and small, separately although this is often ignored except in families. Boil out all vessels and coppers." It seems there was a recognition that Craft Brewing quantities allowed for a better brew.

- Cooling – Pump to coolers. Draw or ladle out of the copper. It should go clear into the coolers. If the cooling is done in an open flat vessel the liquor loses the aromatic part of the hop, "a great deal of the spirit of the liquor is lost." Use a closed vessel.

- Small Beer – Remash and rework goods with hops for 2nd small beer. Add some fresh malt to obtain a 2nd wort nearly as good as the first.

- Yeast – Pitch in winter at the temperature of warm milk, in summer when cooled to room temperature. Make a starter with wort. A thick quart of yeast is right for a hogshead of wort.

- Fermentation – "Increase the fermentation by adding ginger". Commercial brewers use jalap (a purgative). "The Government has attended to the adulteration of bread, it must now do beer. Sieve on fine wheat flour to start a fermentation. Two days should suffice for a fermentation".

- Final course – A bag of bran or 2 or three egg whites beaten up in brandy should be added when the fermentation has ceased (finings).

- Maturing – Again the larger brewers were seen to have the edge. "In fifteen days it should be fine and drunk from the cask. Larger brewers keep this 2 years in casks for the last fermentation. This mellows the drink and the effect is more perfect however the same degree of keeping in any other kind than a brown malt beer would soften it, but take off the spirit. Big brewers correct the faults of one butt of their Porter by means of another, for their judgement directs to mix and bring this to a proper taste and strength".

RECIPE 13. HISTORICAL.

BROWN STOUT. ART AND MYSTERY OF BREWING 1802

Britannica Brown

"As I wish to give every information, take the following extracts from a publication that has been honoured by being copied into Encyclopaedia Britannica. I will say the copyist was no brewer". Fortunately we have the original version, which I believe came from the Art and Mystery of Brewing 1802.

This method does not derive from one gyle but is pieced together from several sources within the same tract. The malt and hop amounts are original as are the mash temperatures, which are quite low for the time.

Original Gravity	1058		15° Plato	
Soft Water	25 litres	23 litres	5 UK gals	5 US gals
West Country Pale	850g kg	780g	1.9 lb.	1.5 lb.
Herts. Pale	1.7 kg	1.57 kg	3.7 lb.	3.3 lb.
Herts. Brown	2.27 kg	2.09 kg	5 lb.	4 lb.
Herts. Amber	2.27 kg	2.09 kg	5 lb.	4 lb.
Start of boil	East Kent yellow Goldings 5% alpha-acid.			
New	90g	80g	3 oz	2.5 oz
Old	90g	80g	3 oz	2.5 oz

Brewing method:
- The liquor was run in at 68°C (155°F). When the tap was set the temperature was 59°C (137°F). The first wort gravity was 1060 (15°P).
- A second mash was run in at 66°C (150°F) settled at 56°C (132°F) and was of gravity 1028 (7°P).
- The wort was run into the underback through the hops, then boiled until the hot break and not more than 20 minutes
- Yeast was pitched at 18°C (64°F). The fermentation lasted 3 days by which time the gravity had dropped to 1039 (10°P). Cleansed into kegs at 21°C (70°F).
- Rouse the head three or four times.

Comments:
- This one is low gravity for the time, but then measuring methods left something to be desired. The worts were physically weighed and then compared in weight to clean water.
- As early as 1760 coriander, molasses, ginger and Spanish Juice were being added for flavour and colour. Coriander was expensive at the time and this was certainly not a money saving stunt. The amounts were tiny and measured in a few ounces in 75 barrels. This gyle was spared these additions.
- We are not told that much about the length of boil. In the preamble it is suggested that 20 minutes is enough, but then there is mention of 45 and 90 minutes. Probably all were done sometime or another.

3.2 THE 19TH CENTURY AND PORTER MALT

We have to make the assumption that the 18th century brown malt was not as dark as that of the 19th century. It may of course not be true. All we can base this on is the fact that early 18th century Porters were brewed with all brown malt and this was not the case by the end of the century. Many 19th century tracts no longer refer to brown malt but to brown or blown malt or just Porter malt. Blown malt is described by Stopes (1885) and Skeate White (1860). Reading Skeate White (appendix 4) tells us immediately why Porter was doomed. The danger to the workers and the malting was considerable, and this if only in terms of fire hazard. No one bothered to measure the long-term effects of breathing the smoke.

This is the summary from *The Historical Companion to House-Brewing (1990 edition)*

"Brown, Blown, Snap or Porter Malt.

I doubt anyone has made this malt commercially in the UK in the last 100 years, but beer made from a similar malt is brewed and most sought after around the area of Nuremberg and Bamberg in Germany. It trades under the names of *Schlenkela,* and *Rauchbier,* respectively. Stopes gives a description of its manufacture in Bishop's Stortford in 1870 which is summarised thus:

"Usually in its preparation, steeping couching and growing are conducted in the ordinary way. Some maltsters give a little less time on the withering floor. (Gentle drying phase.) The corn is then laden on the kiln at a thickness rarely exceeding 1½ inches. The fire consists exclusively of wood, generally of oak, but occasionally of beech. Billet and faggot wood are used. Great skill and care are required to tend the fire and turn the floor. This is done only once and the whole drying is completed in 1 to 2 hours. Moderate heat is maintained at first until the moisture has been largely dissipated, then the fire is made up, and flares and blazes so that no little danger exists of the corn igniting. This renders the work of the kiln man both risky and laborious. The sudden and intense heat causes all the grain which has been properly grown to swell to the extent of 25%, and the nature of the fuel employed communicates very agreeably the empyreumatic properties that distinguish this class of malt."

Another Stopes description comes closer to the current German technique. "The malt is half dried and sprinkled with water which if left about 12 hours, toughens the skin. The corn is spread on wire trays to a depth of 1-2 inches and fired over beech, turning at least every four minutes."

Even though brewers had begun to measure gravities and knew that some techniques yielded poor extract rates, by no means all maltsters dried off the water from the green malt with gentle heat first.

Skeate White's description is reproduced in full in appendix 4.

The Art Of Brewing has the following to report, which relates the economic pressures that the invention of the hydrometer had brought.

"The London market is principally supplied with malts from Berkshire and Herts., and, as the processes of making them are very similar, I will begin with offering a few remarks on them.

These malts are carried through the malt-house in the same manner as pale malts usually are: the four walls of the kiln are perpendicular, so that immediately beneath the floor there is a square room, the fire-place is merely two bars to support the fuel, which, in those counties, is principally bavins, or cleft wood. The malt is kiln-spread, to the depth of about two inches; the full effect of the fire is immediately given, and the grain soon becomes partially charred or burnt. For this reason it must be kept constantly in motion, or it would be totally spoiled were it suffered to remain even a few minutes too long.

Some maltsters, in making brown malt, use the same kiln as they do for pale malts, and, after it is getting out of its first sweating, they take it from the kiln, and lay it in a heap for twenty-four hours; after which it is replaced on the kiln, as before noticed, and, cleft wood being the fuel, It is lit to be removed from the kiln in two or three hours.

In either of these methods, which are pretty similar in the results, there are decidedly some disadvantages: 1st, the sudden action of such violent heat expands the air in the malt with too much rapidity; consequently, an increase of bulk ensues; and, malt being purchased by measure, and not by weight, a loss of from 20 to 25 per cent. is incurred to the consumer.

Blowing is the term applied to this process; and the malt thus produced goes by the name of *blown malt.* Secondly, the saccharine matter is partially dispersed. Hence the extract is deficient in quantity, and not infrequently has an empyreumatic or burnt flavour.

Thirdly, the despatch used in drying a floor of brown malt enables the fraudulent maltster to evade the Excise Duties. This is affected by hurrying the *growing* malt through the house, to avoid having too many floors; thus preventing the due vegetation of the barley, and its conversion into saccharine matter or malt.

Fourthly, in wet seasons the barley is stained and injured, and the price is a temptation to purchase; but the colour which the fire gives to the malt disguises the natural defects.

The richness and mealiness of the pale malt are the criteria of its value in the market; but we can form no judgment of the quality of the brown until we apply the saccharometer: and if, in doing so, we use the proper heats, according to the degree of the colour the malt possesses, we shall not be deceived in the results.

The average samples of malt, thus treated, will yield about 62 lbs.

per quarter, while the average produce of pale malt will be about 78 lbs; a deficiency of three firkins of wort, of 20 lbs. per barrel density, in favour of pale malt. This is a very serious difference, and induced some of the best informed brewers to consider different methods of increasing the density of their worts, which had become thin and light – the advance in the price of malt having compelled them to draw more beer, without increasing the quantity of the grist, in order to meet the advance in material.

They found the most obvious way of doing this was, by lessening the quantity of brown malt, and increasing that of pale, in forming the grist; after which it was to acquire flavour from other ingredients; and, to bring up the complexion, part of which had been thus removed, a colouring matter was introduced; and this article in a short time became so essentially requisite, that a Bill has passed Parliament, allowing the use of colouring matter."

This gives us the whole story of Porter, its rise to economic power and fame, when it was good news to be able to hide imperfect malt and in the absence of accurate weighing machines the advantage to the malt-ster of "blowing" the malt, followed by its demise, as the hydrometer (pioneered by Richardson in 1784; appendix 2) and weigher became widely available, pale malt became more reliable and the pressure was on to substitute brown malt with pale. The introduction of pale malt to Porter created the colouring industry at the turn of the 18th and 19th centuries, typified by the introduction of Wheeler's Patent Black malt and also led to the increasing use of adulterants in an attempt to redress flavour problems. The same author spends some time describing the effects of everything from eastern narcotic berries, tobacco and even opiates to liquorice and salts of copper and iron. And so we move into the century of pale malt Porter brewing. This in itself led to the further deterioration in Porter quality. Had the introduction of pale malt Porter been managed properly, it may have remained the popular drink it once was, but avarice meant that the amounts of pale malt increased, and with it the amounts of colouring. Harwood's strong black bitter beverage became a thin, vinous, brown ale, but one using second-rate hops and probably the least satisfactory of the pale malt production. Pale ale doubtless tasted better. By the middle of the 19th century Amsinck seems to have lost the will to brew Porter. His log is littered with errors and inconsistencies in a way that is not evident when he was dealing with Scottish pale ale or IPA. If the invention of Porter was nothing but a marketing device for Brown Beers and Stouts, it now had to pay the price.

I suggest that if we want genuine Porter or blown malt, we'll have to make it ourselves. A bag of green malt heated in an oven very drastically comes close. A description of making your own green malt in a domestic kitchen is to be found in *The Historical Companion to House-Brewing*. We will also need access to some amber malt, the preparation of which is also described. Some maltings produce a product called brown malt, but the wood-smoke flavour is missing and a few other things besides.

The mashing techniques employed became more and more standardised throughout the century, as breweries increased in size and mechanisation took over. The English hung on to their double mash technique far longer than the Scots. Here is an English recipe from Amsinck, who thought sparging and electricity had little future. He normally railed against parsimony but this gyle had no less than three mashes. No wonder he had had enough!

RECIPE 14. HISTORICAL.

STOCK PORTER PRE-1850 (NO. 12 IN AMSINCK'S LOG).

33/- Session Porter

Amsinck's Porters go down in quality towards the end of his chapter on Brown Beers. This was brewed for the pocket of the brewer. There were three mashes, which actually found their way into this gyle plus a fourth mash for the return wort. Am I glad I'm not in business? It really cannot have been worth the effort.

There are many other concessions to economy. New Pale Malt was supplemented with Old and Old Brown Herts. was exclusively used. I doubt the difference between Old and New Brown is significant, provided the Old has not been allowed to go slack. Therein lies the rub! Without the use of plastic containers I suggest all old malt was slack and cheap beers were a way of getting rid of otherwise unusable stock!

The stretching of new hops with old was (we believe) also done for reasons of economy and definitely affected the nature of the beer. It may not necessarily have been bad.

This gyle was also a massive undertaking of nearly 1000 barrels final volume (36 000 gallons or 144 000 pints). Vessels were built of up to 20 000 barrels but such a monster burst at the Meux Brewery in 1814. Eight brewery workers drowned and houses were swept away on that occasion.

Original Gravity	1057		14.5° Plato	
Soft No. 1	25 litres	23 litres	5 UK gals	5 US gals
Old Norfolk Pale Malt	3.06 kg	2.81 kg	6.7 lb.	5.5 lb
New Norfolk Pale Malt	6.12 kg	5.63 kg	13.5 lb.	10.9 lb.
Old Herts. Brown Malt	1.66 kg	1.53 kg	3.7 lb.	3 lb
Black Malt	310g	280g	11 oz	9 oz
Start of boil	New East Kent yellow Goldings 5% alpha-acid.			
	118g	108g	4oz	3.2oz
Start of Boil	East Kent yellow Goldings Yearlings 5% alpha-acid.			
	117g	107g	3.9 oz	3.2 oz

Brewing method:
- The mash liquor was run into the tun at 67°C (153°F). The goods were mashed 60°C (141°F) and then stood for 1½ hours.
- A second mash was run in at 78°C (173°F) and stood for 1 hour after settling at 69°C (156°F).
- A third mash was run in at 69°C (157°F), settled at 68°C (155°F) and was stood 1 hour.
- The first wort was boiled 1½ hours with all the hops.
- The second wort was boiled for 1½ hours with the hops from the first wort.
- The third wort was boiled 4 ½ hours to reduce the volume, with the hops from the second wort.
- The fermentation started at 21°C (69 ½°F) and rose to 27°C (79°F) within 18 hours
- Fermentation lasted 3 days by which time the gravity had dropped to 1025 (6°P). The head was measured at 14 inches.
- The fermentation was probably not skimmed but cleansed into Pontos.
- 4 days later at a heat of 13°C (55°F) the beer was transferred to vats.

There is no information on fining or conditioning but a cheap beer would have been in the drinker's pot within a month.

Comments:
- One can only assume coal was cheap when this gyle was brewed. We may be certain that the brewer didn't have to do the fetching and stoking for surely any economic advantage to extracting a third mash was lost in boiling 429 barrels for 4 ½ hours. Even then only 34 barrels were actually wasted as steam. Mr. Guinness' notion of driving the brewery steam engine with the third wort doesn't seem so loopy after all. (See recipe 16)
- Any extracted material in the third wort may have been caramelised by the long boil but even after the boil the third wort gravity was only 1028 (7°P). We Craft Brewers have a much easier time. Down the sink with it!
- We always assume the use of old hops in a dark forgiving beer like Porter was for reasons of economy. Ian Hornsey (Brewing) reminds us that Lambics are exclusively made with old hops, which are far higher in polyphenols, have less antibacterial activity and have a softer bittering effect. Worth considering? Probably not! The important point is not the reason for using, but the effect of old hops.

By comparison, here is a Scottish Porter, brewed in Leith on 10th September 1791.

RECIPE 15. HISTORICAL.

HALF A BREWING OF
LEITH PORTER 1791.

Dr. Black's Porter

Many Victorian brewers praise the Porter method adopted by Mr. Richardson, a noted brewer of the 18th century. That doughty researcher of 19th century gyles James Mc Crorie was about to visit the Brewing Archive in Glasgow so he promised to give their copy of Richardson a working-over for me. He found nothing of interest in the body of Richardson's work, but several handwritten sheets were laid inside written by a certain Dr. Black of Edinburgh who recorded some brews he did in Leith in 1791. Black obviously had come by a new fangled Blake's Hydrometer, which measured directly in brewer's gravity units and so he spent many pages describing his experiences with his new toy. This is the first reference to such use I have found.

Everything else was not so easy. I'm sure Dr. Black would have felt the tawse had he written like that at school! His handwriting has left me uncertain about many of his actions, including hop quantities. Dr. Black was also sparging in that year albeit rather half-heartedly. Other snippets to emerge from the pages were about a visit to Whitbread's Brewery where Dr. Black observed they brewed Porter 6 days a week for 8 months of the year using 200 quarters for every 600 barrels. This is made up of three worts, each of 200 barrels, or 3 barrels to the quarter at gravity 65.

Original Gravity	1050		13° Plato	
Soft water	25 litres	23 litres	5 UK gals	5 US gals
Pale Malt	1.77 kg	1.63 kg	3.9 lb.	3.1 lb
Brown	1.77 kg	1.63 kg	3.9 lb.	3.1 lb
Old Amber	1.77 kg	1.63 kg	3.9 lb.	3.1 lb
Start of boil	New East Kent yellow Goldings 5% alpha-acid.			
	154g	142g	5oz	4oz

Brewing method:
- The mash liquor was run into the tun at 71°C (160°F). The goods were mashed 70°C (158°F) and then stood for 1 ½ hours.
- A second mash was run in at 79°C (175°F) and stood for 1 hour after settling at 77°C (170°F).
- The sparge was small, only $\frac{1}{6}$ the size of the two equal mashes.
- There is no information on the boil.
- The fermentation started at 14°C (58°F) and rose to 23°C (73°F) within 2 days by which time the gravity had dropped to 1016 (4°P). The head rose high.
- The fermentation was probably not skimmed but cleansed once the temperature began to drop.
- There is no information on fining or conditioning but although a fairly cheap beer it was kept at least 6 months, when some was decanted into bottles.

Comments:
- The hop quantities are unclear to me. More research needed into the notation (and handwriting), so I've had to guess.
- Like the Amsinck recipe this uses multiple mashes. In the original there are 2 mashes, one sparge (it being Scottish) followed by another 2 mashes. I've only considered the first two mashes, and assumed the other washings were used as a return wort.
- These methods (Amsinck and Black) seem to be typical for the first half of the 19th century, with the mixing of equal quantities of Brown, Amber and Pale malts.
- The other thing we can deduce about Dr. Black is that he was of good Presbyterian stock. He mashed and boiled on Saturday, which left him to ferment on Sunday. Only working on a Sunday would have been considered sufficient reason not to be in Church or at home reading the Bible.

3.3 THE END OF A FASHION

The final question to be answered is, "what is the difference between Porter and Stout in the 19th century?"

At the beginning of the Porter story, back in 1720 something, some very strong Brown Beers were called "Stout Beers" in deference to their strength and blackness. By the end of the century it seems that Brown Beers especially when adulterated were more frequently referred to as Porter. During the first half of the 19th century the word Stout occurs again, maybe simply out of fashion, maybe because one very important brewery in Dublin brewed a Brown Beer of exceptional quality and called it Dublin Stout. By 1850 Porter seems to be being brewed weaker than Stout and so Porter becomes the poor relation. This is best illustrated by the series of Brown Beer gyles reported by my hero Mr. Amsinck. Here a particularly influential one, brewed (probably in London although there is no evidence) in the presence of Mr. Amsinck by one John Guinness.

RECIPE 16. HISTORICAL.
DUBLIN STOUT
(NO. 11 IN THE AMSINCK LOG).

Dublin Stout by Mr. John G. Guinness Jnr.

This brew receives the most attention to detail of any quoted by Amsinck. I include Amsinck's original description in appendix 4. It is worth noting that the Irish, along with the Scots embraced new ideas and technology far more readily than the English Victorian brewers. One senses the reverence in which Amsinck held this great brewer whom he had persuaded to make a demonstration brew of his Irish Stout. Things didn't run to plan for John Guinness and Amsinck's Schadenfreude over the failure of the new fangled ideas is clear to read. One can imagine the dismay when Mr. Guinness, having failed to extract the quantity he though appropriate, kept sparging. He seems to have sparged so much that they were at a loss as to how to boil it. In fact they had to "empty the engine boiler, take the return wort therein, drive the engine with the steam generated therefrom, until it was reduced to a usable quantity!"

No price is mentioned so I assume it never found its way onto the open market.

Original Gravity	1092		23° Plato	
Soft Water No. 2	25 litres	23 litres	5 UK gals	5 US gals
New Suffolk Pale Malt	8.8 kg	8.1 kg	19.4 lb.	15.7 lb
Black Malt	290g	218g	9.5 oz	8 oz
Start of boil	East Kent yellow Goldings 5% alpha-acid.			
	400g	370g	13.5 oz	11 oz

Brewing method:
- The mash liquor was heated to 79°C (175°F) and run into the tun at 76°C (168°F). The goods were mashed for ½ hour at 66°C (150°F) and then infused for 70 minutes.
- A second mash was run in at 83°C (182°F) and stood for 45 minutes after settling at 67°C (153°F).
- A series of complex sparges followed, some very hot, but were used as a return wort.
- The first wort was one half the volume of the second and was boiled 75 minutes.
- The second wort was boiled for 3 hours, presumably to reduce the volume. (If we omit the sparges, this can surely be shortened, our worts boiled as one for the shorter time, with all the hops).
- The fermentation lasted 3 days by which time the gravity had dropped to 1025 (6°P). The temperature was allowed to rise from 16°C (60°F) to 28°C (82°F) during that time. The fermentation was probably not skimmed.
- After 3 days the young beer was cleansed into hogsheads where the yeast seemed to do little and so went into settling backs exactly 6 days after the fermentation was started. Virtually no yeast settled out.
- The gyle was kept in a vat for 6 months and then divided into another.

Comments:

- The grist was then sparged no less than three times with aliquots ranging in temperature between 67°C and 94°C (153 – 202°F). Mr. Guinness seems to have been on a mission to see show how good the conversion would be when done by the Irish. Amsinck remarks (smugly) that Guinness was unsuccessful and much of the return wort was discarded. The second worts and sparges had to be boiled a long time, presumably to achieve the desired starting gravity.

- The depth of head is recorded, achieving 46 inches after 2 ½ days. Amsinck writes, "This Gyle was carried out by Mr. John G. Guinness Jnr., for my instruction. The result was satisfactory, as to flavour, it closely represented the famous Dublin Stout. That peculiar sort of musty flavour, I imagine, is gained by carrying the fermentation, in the square, until the heat and the head drop".

- Not skimming the head during fermentation definitely influences the beer and increases the bittering components retained in the beer.

- A commonly held opinion (Classic Stout & Porter Protz 1997) was that Guinness used roasted barley in their most famous Stout, because it didn't attract the crippling malt tax. There is no mention on roasted barley on this grain bill! A Guinness secret John wasn't prepared to share with Amsinck or another Brewer's Myth?

RECIPE 17. HISTORICAL.

DOUBLE STOUT (NO. 11 CONTINUED IN THE AMSINCK LOG)

Double Stout, Porter by Mr. John G. Guinness

Mr. Guinness was apparently so embarrassed by the malheur with his Dublin Stout that he gave Amsinck this method.

Amsinck wrote, "So much for the Practical information, which I was exceedingly pleased to obtain. The following are written instructions that Mr. Guinness gave me for other Dublin Brown Beer, which I insert, literatim et verbatim."

Although the method is recorded in great detail, there is no information on the quantities. This gyle was eight times the size of the Dublin Stout. I suggest using the same quantities but diluting or boiling less to achieve the lower gravity. The description is so complex that it is anyone's guess if I have really interpreted it correctly.

Original Gravity	1086		22° Plato	
Soft	25 litres	23 litres	5 UK gals	5 US gals
New Suffolk Pale Malt	8.8 kg	8.1 kg	19.4 lb.	15.7 lb
Black Malt	290g	218g	9.5 oz	8 oz
Start of boil	East Kent yellow Goldings 5% alpha-acid.			
	400g	370g	13.5 oz	11 oz

Brewing method:
- The mash liquor was run into the tun at 73°C (165°F). The goods were mashed for ½ hour and then infused for 1 hour having settled at 62°C (144°F).
- More water was added at 78°C (172°F), presumably to keep the mash temperature up.
- A second liquor was run on at 82°C (180°F), mashed 20 minutes, and stood for 45 minutes after settling at 67°C (152°F).
- Dashes of hot water were added at 82-84°C (180 -182°F), and stood 10 minutes.
- The two worts were approximately the same volume. The first was boiled 1 ¼ hours and the second 3 ½ hours, to reduce volume. All the hops seem to have been added at the beginning of the first boil, and then presumably transferred to the second boil.
- The fermentation started at 14°C (58°F) and was roused with a stone of barm to every 10 barrels of gyle. It remained 3 ½ days in the tun by which time the gravity had dropped to 1022 (6°P). The temperature was allowed to rise from 80°F during that time.
- After the barm had been worked off the beer was run into a settling back for 30 hours and then pumped into a maturing vat for 6-8 months.
- The gyle was sent out mixed half old Porter (8 months) and half new Porter (4 months).

Comments:
- The mixing of beers was done in deference to the problems of storing a commodity so long. British brewers were respected throughout the world for their readiness to tie up capital and equipment for such lengths of time. One certainly can't accuse them of this nowadays. A futures market developed in beers. Anyone who had spare warehousing capacity bought a young beer from the trade, stored it up to a year and then sold it back at a huge profit to the breweries as old ale or old Porter. The brewer then mixed it with much younger beer in order to defray some of the profit given to the canny speculator with a warehouse. IPA and best pale ales were not (normally) mixed after storage and were sold properly aged as a premium product.
- A stone of barm is difficult to imagine. Barm is the froth off a fermenting alcoholic drink, usually used to start bread rising. 14lbs of froth seems unlikely so maybe it just meant a fermenting wort, in which case why measure it by weight? Did it refer to a stone jar of working yeast and not a stone in weight? A stone Porter jar of the time is shown on the inside front cover of the book and is marked as holding 6 quarts (1½ gallons)

RECIPE 18. HISTORICAL.

DOUBLE STOUT.

(NO. 3 IN THE AMSINCK LOG).

Double Stout 53/-per barrel

This gyle was brewed in February with soft liquor. In his notes Amsinck writes "Brown Beer Brewed in Season – Stout 30 lbs. Gravity, 160 degrees in the tun, Tap Heat 144 to 145 Degrees, Porter 21 lbs. Gravity, 157 Degrees in the tun, Tap Heat 140 – 144 Degrees, in summer 3 Degrees lower."

Thus by the 1850s (in the opinion of Amsinck) the difference between Stout and Porter was one of strength and mash temperature. Stout beers, as the name suggests, were the stronger and mashed hotter.

He continues, "These heats are for Hard Liquor, Soft requires less by two degrees in the tap heat."

Also of note is the fact that in this gyle Amsinck tells us how many pounds in weight one quarter of each malt type was worth. The error in assuming they all were approximately the same is huge and has caused me to go back and correct much earlier work. The result was a reduction of around 30% in dark malts. I assume that blown malt would weigh even less per quarter. These Victorian Stouts get forever lighter.

Original Gravity	1086		22° Plato	
Soft No. 1	25 litres	23 litres	5 UK gals	5 US gals
Old Pale Malt	7 kg	6.4 kg	15.2 lb.	12.3 lb
New Pale	5.76 kg	5.3 kg	12.7 lb.	10.3 lb.
New Brown	1.63 kg	1.5 kg	3.59 lb.	2.0 lb.
Black Malt	290g	270g	10 oz	8 oz
Start of boil	East Kent yellow Goldings 5% alpha-acid.			
New	203g	186g	6.8 oz	5.5 oz
Yearling	200g	180g	6.7 oz	5.4 oz

Brewing method:
- The mash liquor was run into the tun at 71°C (160°F) and settled at 64°C (147°F). The goods were mashed and then stood 1½ hours.
- A second mash was started at 80°C (176°F), settled at 71°C (159°F) and stood for 1 hour.
- A third mash was carried out but only used as a return wort.
- The two worts were almost the same volume. They were separately boiled for 3 and 6 hours respectively.
- The fermentation lasted 2¼ days by which time the gravity had dropped to 1032 (8°P). The temperature was allowed to rise from 16°C (60°F) to 26°C (78°F). The young beer was not skimmed and the head is given as 18 inches.
- After this time it was cleansed into pontos and then put into a vat 3 days later. There is no information about the gravity.
- No information on storage or sale is provided.

Comments:
- We don't know in what proportion and when the hops were added to the boil. The second wort was boiled for 6 hours, presumably to reduce the volume and increase the colour by caramalisation of whatever sugars were in the second wort.
- The hop amounts are roughly the same as for his treble Stout but in the interest of economy 50% old hops were used. This may be uncharitable of me. Perhaps the altered flavour of old hops was desired and not introduced out of parsimony, viewed by some as an Amsinck foible. Most brewers reduced the hop amounts in Brown Beers. This gyle may not have been all that dark (only one third brown and black malt) and thus the hops not wasted as would have been the case in a black 18th century Stout.
- Amsinck defines the difference between Stout and Porter in terms of gravity and mash-tun heats. "BROWN BEER BREWED IN SEASON – Stout 30 lbs. gravity, 160 Degrees in tun, Tap Heat 144 to 145 Degrees, Porter 21 lbs. gravity, 157 Degrees in tun, Tap Heat 140 to 142 Degrees, in summer 3 Degrees lower." (Appendix 11).

RECIPE 19. HISTORICAL.

TREBLE STOUT.

(NO. 2 IN THE AMSINCK LOG).

Treble Stout 63/-per barrel
This brew is only exceeded in detail by the abortive John Guinness brew.
Amsinck was quite dismissive of the Scottish sparge and whenever possible
stuck to the old multiple mashes. This is a reminder that mash originally meant
the time spent stirring the grist with the mash liquor. The infusion time is covered by such terms as "rested" or "stood". Nowadays "mash" refers to the useful time spent converting starch to sugar and includes the period of stirring and
resting. When Amsinck writes "second mash" he is really extracting material by
stirring with hot water and this was instead of sparging. Durden Park members
have tested and compared sparging with multiple mashing and can detect little
qualitative or quantitative difference.

Original Gravity	1094		24° Plato	
Soft No. 2	25 litres	23 litres	5 UK gals	5 US gals
New Pale Malt	8.54 kg	7.86 kg	18.8 lb.	15.2 lb
New Brown	2 kg	1.9 kg	4.55 lb.	3.7 lb.
Black Malt	250g	230g	9 oz	5 oz
Start of boil	East Kent yellow Goldings 5% alpha-acid.			
	500g	450g	16.5 oz	13.5 oz

Brewing method:
- The mash liquor was heated to 77°C (170°F) and run into the tun at 71°C (160°F). The goods settled at 64°C (147°F) after mashing and then stood 2 hours.
- A second mash was started at 82°C (180°F), settled at 71°C (160°F) and stood for 90 minutes
- A series of complex sparges followed but were only used as return worts.
- The second wort was almost double the volume of the first. They were separately boiled for 3 and 2 hours respectively.
- The fermentation lasted barely 36 hours by which time the gravity had dropped to 1044 (11°P). The temperature was allowed to rise from 17°C to 24°C (63°F to 76°F). The young beer was cleansed into pontos and then put into a vat four days later, by which time it was 1033 (8°P).
- No information on storage or sale is provided.

Comments

- We don't know in what proportion and when the hops were added to the boil. The second wort was boiled for 3 hours, presumably to reduce the volume. If we reduce the volume of the second mash then the worts can be combined and the boil shortened, with all the hops. However, long boils alter the nature of a Brown Beer, by increasing caramalisation.

- The hop amounts may be viewed by some as an Amsinck foible. Most brewers reduced the hop amounts in Brown Beers. This gyle may not have been all that dark (only one third brown and black malt) and thus the hops considered necessary.

- Bickerdyke supposes that the excessive sparges used had the effect of leaching some of the bitter husk material into the Porter wort and as such contributed to the "Porter" taste.

RECIPE 20. HISTORICAL.

COUNTRY PORTER

(PAGE 61 OF AMSINCK LOG).

Country Porter

Country Porter receives also one paragraph and is quite confused in its content. "The only difference to Dublin Stout, is the temperature of the kives, the same as Dublin Stout." Amsinck was normally so exact. Perhaps he had had enough of Irish recipes. The point is that we don't know how much credence to give to Town and Country Porters.

I have included this material because it shows that even in the mid 19th century there was no homogenous behaviour in society. We live in times in which we can buy almost any commodity anywhere in the country. It wasn't always so.

Country Porter (according to Amsinck) was a tad stronger than the town version, but nearly double the hopping rate. It wasn't mixed prior to sale.

Original Gravity	1067		17° Plato	
Soft No. 2	25 litres	23 litres	5 UK gals	5 US gals
New Suffolk Pale Malt	6.4 kg	5.9 kg	14.1 lb.	11.4 lb
Black Malt	210g	193g	6.9 oz	5.8 oz
Start of boil	East Kent yellow Goldings 5% alpha-acid.			
	200g	180g	6.7 oz	5.4 oz

Brewing method:

- The mash liquor was heated to 79°C (175°F) and run into the tun at 76°C (168°F). The goods were mashed for ½ hour at 66°C (150°F) and then infused for 70 minutes.
- A second mash was run in at 83°C (182°F) and stood for 45 minutes after settling at 67°C (153°F).
- The first wort was one half the volume of the second and was boiled 1$\frac{1}{4}$ hours.
- The second wort was boiled for 3 hours, presumably to reduce the volume.
- The fermentation lasted 3 days by which time the gravity had dropped to 1025 (6°P). The yeast was pitched and the fermentation kept at 27°C (80°F) for 46 hours.
- The fermentation was probably not skimmed but stood in the settling back for 30 hours.
- The beer was transferred to a vat and kept a day or two before fining.

- Comments:
- The use of finings may indicate that this Porter went straight to the publican and was served within a week to a fortnight. Amsinck's own brews were never fined and normally kept at least 6 months.
- As mentioned, one of the few literary references to Porter occurs in Jane Austen's Sense and Sensibility. Maybe this was close to what Mr. Willoughby drank in that Marlborough inn. It did the trick for all the sisters enjoyed a happy ending.

RECIPE 21. HISTORICAL.

TOWN PORTER

(PAGE 61 OF AMSINCK LOG).

Town Porter

Town Porter receives but one paragraph and may have been a general way of making and serving Porter in Amsinck's locality or may have been a quirk. It does seem as though this method had the blessing of Mr. Guinness, (which one may argue counts for nothing after the fiasco with the steam engine). It is certainly a derivative of Dublin Stout and thus is Irish in origin. If served promptly it must have had a suspicion of sweetness from the 10% fresh worts. It also enjoys hopping rates only around 10% of true Dublin Stout. There is no information on the price per barrel it fetched.

Original Gravity	1064		16° Plato	
Soft No. 2	25 litres	23 litres	5 UK gals	5 US gals
New Suffolk Pale Malt	6.1 kg	5.6 kg	13.5 lb.	15.7 lb
Black Malt	200g	183g	6.6 oz	5.5 oz
Start of boil	East Kent yellow Goldings 5% alpha-acid.			
	110g	100g	3.5 oz	3 oz

Brewing method:
- The mash liquor was heated to 79°C (175°F) and run into the tun at 76°C (168°F). The goods were mashed for ½ hour at 66°C (150°F) and then infused for 70 minutes.
- A second mash was run in at 83°C (182°F) and stood for 45 minutes after settling at 67°C (153°F).
- The first wort was one half the volume of the second and was boiled 75 minutes.
- The second wort was boiled for 2 ½ hours, presumably to reduce the volume.
- The fermentation lasted 3 days by which time the gravity had dropped to 1028 (7°P). The yeast was pitched and the fermentation kept at 26°C (78°F) for 42 hours.
- The fermentation was probably not skimmed but stood in the settling back for 30 hours.
- The beer was transferred to a vat and kept one further day before mixing thus:

Young Porter	25 litres	23 litres	5 UK gallons	5 US gallons
Fresh worts	2.5 litres	2.3 litres	4 pints	4 pints
Dublin Stout	830 ml	760 ml	1 ⅓ pints	1 ⅓ pints

Finings were then used and this may indicate that this Porter went straight to the publican and was served within a week to a fortnight.

Comments:
- We learn from this recipe a new piece of brewing jargon, which my Irish Craft Brewing friends could have taught me: the Irish word for a mash tun was a kive.
- We have already mentioned the developing futures market in beer. This seems to be a way of getting round the re-purchase of a gyle, warehoused by someone else and then sold back to the brewery at a huge profit. The amount of mature Dublin Stout in the final beer was about $1/30$ the amount of new Porter. Again Porter seems to be synonymous by the 1850s with a reduction in quality.

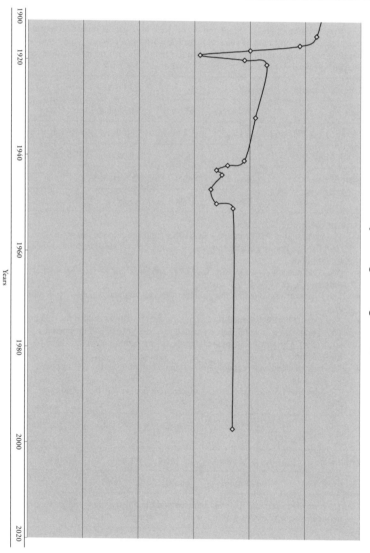

20th Century average beer gravities

RECIPE 22. HISTORICAL.

RUNNING PORTER
(NO. 12 IN AMSINCK'S LOG).

36/- Madras Porter

It is rare to find the use of sugar in any Amsinck report. I'm sure he disapproved, but then when reading the love and attention he paid to his pale ales compared to Brown Beers, I don't think his heart was in Porter brewing. There are all sorts of proof reading errors, which don't occur in the sections on pale beers. For example this recipe asks for "Madras sugar". Surely a misprint! Was his mind was still on his brother in Madras, to whom he regularly sent IPA? Did he mean Demerara or Madeira perhaps?

Fighting the Porter corner had become an unequal battle by the time Amsinck sent his log to the printers. Beer quality was on its way down and many brewers were making Porter as black and bitter as they could get it, probably to cover a multitude of sins and probably using colouring, not brown malt. It all ended in tears with the demise of the dark beer trade. 150 years later I have scoured the supermarket shelves for anything worth reporting. Where has all the flavour gone?

Original Gravity	1064		16° Plato	
Hard No. 8	25 litres	23 litres	5 UK gals	5 US gals
New Pale Malt	4.72 kg	4.34 kg	10.4 lb.	8.4 lb
New Brown Malt	1.31 kg	1.21 kg	2.8 lb.	2.3 lb
Black Malt	870g	800g	1.9 lb.	1.6 lb.
Madras Sugar	330g	300g	11 ½ oz	9 ½ oz
Start of boil	New East Kent yellow Goldings 5% alpha-acid.			
	118g	108g	4oz	3.2oz
Start of Boil	East Kent yellow Goldings Yearlings 5% alpha-acid.			
	117g	107g	3.9 oz	3.2 oz

Brewing method:
- The mash liquor was run into the tun at 68°C (154°F). The goods were mashed 141°F and then stood for 2 hours.
- The grain was sparged at 82°C (180°F) and then stood ½ hour (to drain?). This first wort was sent to the boiler and boiled with all the hops for 1 hour.
- A second mash was run in at 80°C (176°F), mashed and stood for 1 hour after settling at 69°C (156°F).
- The second wort was boiled for 2 hours with the hops from the first wort.
- The third wort was boiled 4 ½ hours to reduce the volume, with the hops from the second wort.
- The fermentation started at 17°C (62°F) and was roused after 12 hours.
- The temperature rose to 24°C (75°F) by which time the gravity had dropped to 1033 (8°P).
- The fermentation was probably not skimmed but cleansed into hogsheads.
- 3 days later at a heat of 20°C (68°F) the beer was racked into casks for delivery.

There is no information on fining or conditioning. This may have been served as soon as it had settled in the publican's cellar.

Comments:
- As mentioned, this method is riddled with mistakes. The original text uses the days of the week to describe the progress of the fermentation. Unfortunately the type-setter got carried away with the ditto signs and forgot to put the days in. Thus it reads as though the complete fermentation was carried out on a Saturday and was finished before it started.

I suggest the following amendments:

Fermentation:

Day	Time	Temperature	Gravity	Actions
Saturday	7 a.m.	17°C (62°F)	23 lbs	
	6 p.m.	19°C (65°F)	18.4 lbs	Roused
Sunday	10 p.m.	19°C (65°F)	17.2 lbs	
Tuesday	6 a.m.	24°C (75°F)	11.6 lbs	
	?	20°C (68°F)		Cleansed into Hogsheads
Wednesday	Racked into casks for delivery			

- The typesetter wasn't the only problem! There was no refrigeration available and although the gyle was a minnow by Victorian standards (11 ¼ barrels), they couldn't get the heat down from 68°F, which was considered far too warm. It was common to have refrigerated settling backs by then.

3.4 THE DEMISE OF PORTERS AND STOUTS

Amsinck was determined to preserve the balance of brown and pale malt. Unfortunately we only know when his records were published, not when the actual brewings took place. I suspect that most were done in the early years of the 19th century. I base this on the fact that he gives all his gravities in lbs/barrel. This means he physically weighed the worts and didn't have use of a suitable brewer's hydrometer. He was also anti-sparge, a position which would not have been tenable in commercial brewing after around 1840.

Towards the end of the century things rapidly deteriorated and brown malt was rapidly disappearing from the grain schedules. The 1863 edition of *The Brewer* didn't try to halt the trend; there was no point, but did provide advice for brewers who still wanted to brew a genuine Porter using brown malt instead of pale with black for colouring. The following table of malt ratios was provided for a 20 quarter brewing. Of course we can substitute kilograms or pounds weight or whatever. It is the ratio that is important.

Gyle	Pale	Brown	Amber	Black	Pale:(Brown):Black
1	12	7		1	12:(7):1
2	18			2	9:1
3			19	1	
4	9	5	5	1	9:(5):1
5	11 ½	6	2	½	23:(12):1

The 18:2 ratio (gyle 2) would hardly have produced a rich rounded mellow Porter although the rider is added that the black malt must be properly prepared. This meant, "start as if for pale malt, dry carefully and then carefully roast". The inference is that much black malt was made from reject pale!

We are also given some hop values. A Kent variety called *Humulus Germanicus* is recommended as being well adapted for Porter Brewing, requiring 8-10 months to mellow and providing a "soft full peculiar bitter enhanced by keeping". 8 or 9 lbs hops per quarter of malt are recommended for domestic Porter and 10 lbs for export. This is impossible to accurately convert, the quarter being a measure of volume but I estimate it at 3 ounces hops per 5 lbs malt (180g per 5 kilos). Hops were often steeped several hours in hot water at 60-77°C (140-170°F) prior to use!

There is also information on recommended mash heats and no mention is made of sparging even as late as 1863! *The Brewer* writes:

"The mode of extracting Porter Wort does not differ from that recommended in brewing ale, except that additional mashing may be requisite to reduce the pasty consistency and insoluble parts of the high-dried corn, especially of the black malt, when the latter is mixed in the tun.

The mashing heat should be low as low heats produce brighter worts."

For a treble mash extract he suggests 70°C, 80 and, 87°C (158 176 and 188°F) and for four mashes, 73, 80, 82 and 88°C (158, 164, 180 and 190°F). This is academic for modern craft brewers who are not interested in return worts for the next day's mash liquor but the figures help us to understand the thinking when formulating gyles. The third and fourth worts were not always used as return worts in Brown Beer brewing but were often boiled to bring their gravities up to the level of the combined first and second worts, then added to these worts for boiling with the hops, which never exceeded 90 minutes.

The yeast was pitched at 16-21°C (60-70°F) and the fermentation heat curbed at less than 27°C (80°F). Cleansing was carried out at around 1032 (8°P). Filling into casks was undertaken at 1020 (5°P). Export Porter was treated in much the same way as other export beers. This involved vatting for at least ten months, and then opening again for three or four weeks to be sure there was no residual gas. It was clarified and bunged with cane bungs owing to their porosity.

Of more interest is not what the learned were urging brewers to do, but what the brewers were actually doing. Fortunately the Durden Park Beer Circle have taken it upon themselves to actually work up the brewery records. Here is a Durden Porter, actually brewed just before the 1863 edition of *The Brewer*. I leave you to make the comparison.

RECIPE 23. HISTORICAL.

FROM DR. J. HARRISON'S RESEARCH AT THE WHITBREAD BREWING ARCHIVE.

Whitbread's London Porter 1850.
"One of the circles favourite beers," is all they write.
The ratio of grains is high on pale and low on brown when compared to The Brewer of 1863, but the difference between this gyle and the 12:7:1 is not enormous.
My thanks go to members of the Durden Park Beer Circle in West London for allowing me to use their work.

Original Gravity	1060		15° Plato	
No analysis.	25 litres	23 litres	5 UK gallons	5 US gallons
Pale Malt	3.2 kg	2.94 kg	6.3 lbs	5.1 lbs
Black Malt	400g	370g	13 oz	10 oz
Brown Malt	1.12 kg	1.03 kg	2.2 lbs	1.8 lbs
Copper & Dry	Fuggles or Goldings 4 – 5% alpha–acid.			
Copper	150g	140g	5 oz	4 oz
Dry hops	3g		0.1 oz	

Brewing method:
- Add hot water to the ground grain to produce a stiff mash at 66°C (150°F)
- Maintain this temperature for 180 minutes.
- Raise the temperature to 77°C (170°F) for 30 minutes.
- Sparge slowly with water at 82–85°C (182–185°F) to obtain the required volume.
- Boil with hops for 90 minutes.
- Cool, strain and rinse the hops.
- Adjust to the required gravity by adding cold boiled water or dried pale malt extract as needed.
- Ferment with a good quality ale yeast.
- Dry hop with $^1/_{10}$ oz (3g) Goldings.
- Mature for at least 4 months.

Comments:
- Whitbread were a large brewery in the 1850s producing prolific amounts of beer. They were market leaders in terms of volume and the Durden Park members obviously felt good about this Porter. This may be as typical as one can get for the 1850s but I would recommend doubling the amount of Brown Malt.

By comparison to the Whitbread Stout, William Black's Brown Stout barely pays lip service to Brown Malt. Nevertheless it earns the Durden accolade.

RECIPE 24. HISTORICAL.

RESEARCHED AND WORKED UP BY

DURDEN PARK BEER CIRCLE

William Black's Brown Stout 1849
"A mouth filling strong Scottish Porter, with a soft roast grain flavour" is the circle's comment.
No doubt The Brewer of 1863 would have disapproved. The question is one of expectation. Durden research shows there was a strong market in good low brown-malt Porters, very much ignoring the historical precedent.
My thanks go to members of the Durden Park Beer Circle in West London for allowing me to use their work.

Original Gravity	1072		18° Plato	
No analysis.	25 litres	23 litres	5 UK gallons	5 US gallons
Pale Malt	2.81 kg	2.59 kg	5.5 lbs	4.5 lbs
Black Malt	200g	180g	6.5 oz	5 oz
Brown Malt	180g	160g	0.3 lbs	0.25 lbs
Amber Malt	2.81 kg	2.59 kg	5.5 lbs	4.5 lbs
Copper & Dry	Fuggles or Goldings 4 – 5% alpha–acid.			
Copper	268g	246g	9 oz	7.5 oz
Dry hops	3g		0.1 oz	

Brewing method:
- Add hot water to the ground grain to produce a stiff mash at 66°C (150°F)
- Maintain this temperature for 180 minutes.
- Raise the temperature to 77°C (170°F) for 30 minutes.
- Sparge slowly with water at 82–85°C (182–185°F) to obtain the required volume.
- Boil with hops for 90 minutes.
- Cool, strain and rinse the hops.
- Adjust to the required gravity by adding cold boiled water or dried pale malt extract as needed.
- Ferment with a good quality ale yeast.
- Dry hop with $1/10$ oz (3g) Goldings.
- Mature for at least 6 months.

Comments:
- This gyle used very little brown malt and very little colouring. It was well hopped and I'm sure an excellent beer. Was it Porter? If nothing else we see what a nonsense beers styles are.
- I would recommend four times the amount of Brown Malt.
- This brew would also be suitable for making an oyster Stout. Stouts were served as the perfect foil to seafoods. Some breweries added oyster flesh to the boil.

Things go from bad to worse as we progress through the 19th century. Here is an Usher's Brew from 1885, now using dark and pale crystal malts and a high pale to black ratio of 9:1. Still just about acceptable.

RECIPE 25. HISTORICAL.

FROM DR. J. HARRISON'S RESEARCH INTO SCOTTISH BREWING LEDGERS, HERIOT WATT UNIVERSITY.

Usher's Stout 1885.
"A typical full-bodied Victorian Stout," is the description. There is plenty to pull a face about. Crystal malt, which dominates much modern beer makes an appearance as does brown sugar, which colours and adds alcohol but has little else apart from cheapness to recommend it. Brown malt just about gets onto the grain schedule.

My thanks go to members of the Durden Park Beer Circle in West London for allowing me to use their work.

Original Gravity	1056		14° Plato	
No analysis.	25 litres	23 litres	5 UK gallons	5 US gallons
Pale Malt	2.88 kg	2.65 kg	5.6 lbs	4.6 lbs
Black Malt	640g	590g	1.25 lbs	1 lbs
Crystal Malt	320g	290g	0.6 lbs	0.5 lbs
Brown sugar	320g	290g	0.6 lbs	0.5 lbs
Carapils	1.04 kg	960g	2 lbs	1.6 lbs
Amber Malt	320g	290g	0.6 lbs	0.5 lbs
Brown Malt	320g	290g	0.6 lbs	0.5 lbs
Copper & Dry	Fuggles 4 – 5% alpha–acid.			
Copper	150g	140g	5 oz	4 oz
Dry hops	3g		0.1 oz	

Brewing method:
- Add hot water to the ground grain to produce a stiff mash at 66°C (150°F)
- Maintain this temperature for 180 minutes.
- Raise the temperature to 77°C (170°F) for 30 minutes.
- Sparge slowly with water at 82–85°C (182–185°F) to obtain the required volume.
- Boil with hops for 90 minutes.
- Cool, strain and rinse the hops.
- Adjust to the required gravity by adding cold boiled water or dried pale malt extract as needed.
- Ferment with a good quality ale yeast.
- Dry hop with $1/_{10}$ oz (3g) Goldings.
- Mature for 4 months.

Comments:
- Fuggles in the copper from the beginning of the boil is unusual at that time. Breweries rarely were specific about variety and it would be interesting to know if this is Durden Park deciding to have a change from Goldings or if Fuggles were specified.
- The amounts of amber and brown are very low, reflecting the economy thinking of a large late 19th century brewery. "Use pale malt and colouring" were the bywords and led to malts such as carapils, which is actually pale crystal malt and can be used to replace amber. (Tush).

The twentieth century is the time for all sorts of adulterations again. Not poisonous and not necessarily deleterious; it all depends on the taste buds. However, they are all brewed too pale, too few hops, and not enough brown malt bite, except perhaps Guinness, but I'm told that is but a pale imitation of what used to be. Oyster Stout, chocolate Stout, (due to the malt of that name), and here an oatmeal Stout from 1905, which is late and unauthentic enough for me.

RECIPE 26. HISTORICAL.

FROM DR. J. HARRISON'S RESEARCH, HERIOT WATT UNIVERSITY.

Maclay's Oatmeal Stout 1909.

"A chewy, satisfying Stout," is the terse description that this beer earns. The word "oatmeal" can be supplied from plain unadulterated breakfast oats. This doesn't quite get into the 19th century nor is it Victorian by 6 years and has already cast off the shackles of brown malt. This one works apparently or else Durden Park wouldn't have entertained it but it is a pale malt job with colouring. The use of amber is 19th century but here it is in such tiny amounts as to be insignificant. Its gravity is looking firmly into the 20th century too.

My thanks go to members of the Durden Park Beer Circle in West London for allowing me to use their work.

Original Gravity	1046		12° Plato	
No analysis.	25 litres	23 litres	5 UK gallons	5 US gallons
Pale Malt	3.2 kg	2.94 kg	6.25 lbs	5.06 lbs
Amber Malt	320g	290g	0.6 lbs	0.5 lbs
Black Malt	640g	590g	1.25 lbs	1 lbs
Oats	1.92 kg	1.76 kg	3.75 lbs	3.04 lbs
Copper & Dry	Goldings 5% alpha–acid.			
Copper	150g	140g	5 oz	4 oz
Dry hops	3g		0.1 oz	

Brewing method:
- Mix the oats with boiling water (2 pints) and stand for 10 minutes before mixing with the malts.
- Add hot water to the ground grain to produce a stiff mash at 68°C (155°F)
- Maintain this temperature for 180 minutes.
- Raise the temperature to 77°C (170°F) for 30 minutes.
- Sparge slowly with water at 82–85°C (182–185°F) to obtain the required volume.
- Boil with hops for 90 minutes.
- Cool, strain and rinse the hops.
- Adjust to the required gravity by adding cold boiled water or dried pale malt extract as needed.
- Ferment with a good quality ale yeast.
- Dry hop with $1/_{10}$ oz (3g) Goldings.
- Mature for at least 3 months.

Comments:
- It will be difficult to dry hop with so little material. Don't be tempted to miss it out though. It will make a difference.

RECIPE 27. HISTORICAL.

MACLAY'S PATENT DISCOVERED AND PUT AT MY DISPOSAL BY JAMES MC CRORIE.

Oat Malt Stout (that is to say Porter) 1895.
Our brewer was uncertain if this was Stout or Porter. It is even more unusual for a brewer to patent a recipe. New malts and their production were often the subject of patent but the use of a malt in a brew? This may be unique.

Original Gravity	1046		12° Plato	
No analysis.	25 litres	23 litres	5 UK gallons	5 US gallons
Oat Malt	5.11 kg	4.14 kg	10 lbs	8.1 lbs
Pale Malt	850g	690g	1.7 lbs	1.4 lbs
Amber Malt	430g	350g	0.8 lbs	0.7 lbs
Caramel	570g	460g	1.1 lbs	0.9 lbs
Sugar	280g	230g	0.6 lbs	0.5 lbs
Liquorice	130g	100g	2.5 oz	2.2 oz
Ground linseeds	36g	30g	1 oz	1 oz
Copper	Goldings 5% alpha–acid.			
Copper	140g	120g	4.5 oz	4 oz

Brewing method:
- No precise brewing instructions were given with the patent. Some brewers soaked their oat malt in water overnight to soften it and allow sufficient access to the liquor. Many mashed cold although I think that a step mash at 35°C, 55°C and 65°C would be a good idea, resting 45 minutes at each temperature.
- Maclay claims to have provided instructions somewhere, but at this time I have not discovered there whereabouts.

Comments:
- This is a final bit of research for my readers. Work up a method suitable for this oat malt Stout and I'll include it in future editions of this book and in Brewers' Contact.

The 20th & 21st Centuries

4.1 THE EXCUSES

The 20th century will be remembered for the motor car, moon landings, microprocessors and...excuses.

No Stout Beer or Porter should be brewed with an original gravity below 1065, if it is to have anything to do with the 18th and 19th century concept of a Stout Beer. I looked quickly through The Real Ale Almanac by Roger Protz, and remember Roger and CAMRA are committed to quality. Here are a few random discoveries. I opened a page with my eyes shut and then moved forward through the text to the next Porter or Stout. How random is that?

Brewery	Name	OG	Brown malt (%)
Hesket (Newmarket)	Great Cockup Porter	1035	0 (Pale, crystal, chocolate)
Dyffryn Clwyd	Jolly Jack Tar Porter	1045	0 (Pale, chocolate, roasted barley)
Spinghead (Burton)	Hole-in-Spire Porter	1040	0 (Pale, roasted barley)
Hanby Ales (Wem)	Shropshire Stout	1044	0 (Pale, crystal, black, chocolate)
Crouch Vale (Chelmsf'd)	Essex Porter	1050	0 (Pale, crystal, roasted barley)
Ringwood	XXXX Porter	1048	0 (Pale, crystal/chocolate, torrefied wheat)
Featherstone (Leics)	Stout	1037	0 (Pale, wheat , black)
Larkins (Edenbridge)	Porter	1053	0 (Pale, crystal, chocolate)
Caledonian (Edinburgh)	Porter	1042	0 (Pale, crystal, amber, chocolate, wheat)

The taster's comments are equally revealing.

- Great Cockup as "intriguing" which I assume is CAMRA-speak for "aptly named."
- Essex Porter was described as "authentic, rich and smooth."
- Featherstone Stout is "full tasting and unusually spicy", (and may be close to 50% wheat malt).
- Caledonian is "a delectable dark brew, a fine member of the new Stout breed."

This last comment about Caledonian is honest and to the point. This is a new drink and has nothing to do with the traditional Stout and Porter brewing in the British Isles. But as we have seen, Porter was all things to all men and women.

The drop in gravity that has been witnessed over the last 100 years is due to the high taxation on alcohol. The easiest way to reduce pump prices at the bar is to put less alcohol in the beer. This started in the 1914-18 Great War. Lloyd George had his roots in Chapel Wales and Protz (*Classic Stouts & Porter 1997*) asserts Lloyd George was more than happy to see laws restricting the sale of beer, if it affected the war effort. Interestingly no one told the breweries to brew thinner. That was their own idea, maybe prompted by malt being in short supply (in both wars) because of the shortage of firing material. Breweries made huge profits during the war years because they were *forced* to sell thin beer. They weren't forced to keep the price up, nor continue selling thin beer when the austerity was over and gravities did climb again between the wars.

I took a dozen random best bitter gravities from Protz (*The Real Ale Almanac 5th Ed.* 1997) and found the average was 1037. Placed along with data collected by Monckton (*History of English Ale and Beer* 1966) 20th century trends are clear. See graph on page 125.

Both World wars show a clear reduction in gravity but note how slowly we are recovering from the 1947 low.

And maybe it is right and proper that pubs don't sell beers of the strength of yesteryear. It is no longer socially acceptable to drink and drive or to return to work after a pub lunch, the worse for wear. Therefore there is a place for these Brown Beers brewed at 1035. We have seen that throughout history everyman and his dog brewed a Brown Beer and called it Porter! Why should the 20th and 21st centuries break with that tradition? The traditional Brown Beer brewer still has the option of calling his beer a Stout Beer, or something similar. The craft brewer still has the option of looking at this book or the Durden Park publications, and brewing a proper Brown Beer with colour and strength. It can be enjoyed at home in complete safety. Maybe pubs are there to provide the ambience and craft brewers to provide the nutritional historically correct beverage.

Where does this leave the home brewer, who wants to make a Brown Beer like the one in the pub? Fortunately the *Real Ale Almanac* and *Classic Stout & Porter*, both by Roger Protz, have details of the grain bill, colour and bittering. Most of Roger's work has been summarised by Les Howarth (*The Home Brewer's Recipe Database)*, which is available electronically, so we can search easily for that elusive brew. It is then a case of formulating a recipe and there are plenty of books on the market to tell us how to do that. Furthermore the American Homebrewer's Association has an extract, colour and bittering wheel, in their catalogue which enables us to read off what we will get for a particular malt and bittering hop. For those who don't want to buy a second book, here are some thoughts on formulation.

4.2 THE EXTRACT

Most of the extract comes from pale malts. You should be able to get available extract data from the malting that supplied the malt. If you can't, change your supplier. Remember that maltings test the available extract under ideal conditions and it is in their (marketing) interest to provide a high value. We have to be realistic and allow for the fact we may get 10% less than the quoted figure.

Fawcett's of Castleford have produced a table of their extracts and colours (appendix 9). Their Pale Malt is given as about 300 litre degrees per kg.

This means that
- 1 kg pale malt in 1 litre mash liquor should provide 300 degrees of extract.
- 10 kg pale malt in 1 litre mash should provide 3000 degrees of extract
- 10 kg pale malt in 10 litre mash should provide 300 degrees of extract
- 10 kg pale malt in 50 litre final volume should provide 60 degrees of extract, or 1060 as we would call it.

I usually achieve 1055, with which I'm more than happy, as I don't sparge to the extent of a parsimonious brewery.

Les Howarth summarises the argument thus:

$$\text{Total weight of malt required} = \frac{100 \times (\text{target OG-1000}) \times \text{target volume (litres)}}{300 \times \text{percentage mash efficiency}}$$

4.3 COLOUR

It is not possible to get the colour and the extract right at the same time, unless you have exactly the same ingredients as the original brewer. Colour is expressed in EBC (European Brewing Congress) although US books may still use Lovibond. It is useful to consider colour when deciding on how much dark malt to use. Take care! Crystal malt can come in many shades, varying from very white to black as the night. The impact of crystal malt on the beer is enormous. You must know the EBC value from the maltster, but it is better to stick to the amounts given by the recipe, rather than fool around trying to achieve a particular colour.

Lovibond and EBC colour charts are available for brewers and it is a simple procedure to compare a standard cell full or the finished beer to the colour chart. By doing this we build up experience for the future and that is really the best guide to getting it right. (Whoops! We've come full circle back to *empiricism).*

4.4 BITTERING

Formulations really begin to get hit and miss when dealing with bittering. The alpha acid value on the hop packet is a guide. However:

- two different hop strains with the same alpha acid percentage will not produce the same effect on the beer.
- alpha acid values are measured before sale. They alter as the hops age, especially if they are not foil packed.
- different brewers, using different water and length of boil achieve different utilization rates. Unless we have some of our past successes analysed, we have no way of knowing what our utilization rate is. In this country one normally settles for a figure of around 20%. In the US they assume greater usage. Are we long or short boilers? Do we add all the bittering hop in one go or add them a little at a time? It all makes a difference.

This is the formula provided by Les Howarth in *The Home Brewer's Recipe Database.* It seems generally accepted when working in European units.

$$\text{Weight of hops} = \frac{10 \times \text{volume brewed in litres} \times \text{IBU}}{\text{Alpha acid \% } \times \text{Utilisation \%}}$$

When I started this book I had assumed that modern breweries would part with information about their mash temperature, length, ingredients, boil, fermentation temperature etc.etc. In fact, not one brewery answered my request for information on modern Stouts and Porters. This may have been because they haven't the time to carry the detail from the brewing register to the form I sent them, which would be at least 15 minutes work, or they simply don't want to support the craft brewer.

4.5. MODERN MASHING TECHNIQUES

- Most craft brewers use a mash tun with a perforated false bottom, called a lauter screen in the US, (from the German *läutern,* meaning to clarify).
- A <u>strike temperature</u> of around 75°C (168°F) is chosen, depending on the ambient temperature of the brewery. When the malt is run into the mash liquor the temperature should settle between 62-65°C (144-148°F). Most modern dark beer brewers would err on the low side.
- A <u>mash time</u> of around 60-90 minutes would be correct.
- <u>Sparging</u> is done with a rotating arm and water between 75-85°C (166-188°F). Don't over sparge. The gravity of the prime wort and sparge should be about your target gravity. I stop sparging when the run-off is around 1035.
- Only boil until the hot break occurs. This should not exceed 90 minutes. Most modern brewers add a variety of hops at different points in the boil.

For step by step instructions I would follow the method recommended by the Durden Park Beer Circle, and paraphrased in recipe 24.

4.6 SOME MODERN RECIPES

The following are from a quick trawl through *The Real Ale Almanac.* The types of pale malt are often given but it is quite an exercise to get anything but Marris Otter these days. Remember crystal malt can be many shades. The very dark can give a beautiful nutty flavour, but used in excess produces a wicked cloying sensation

Beer	Fuller's London Porter	Adnams Oyster Stout	Ringwood XXXX Porter	Sweet Stout
Grain	Pale Malt 76% Crystal 10% Brown 12% Chocolate 2%	Pale malt 70% Crystal 10% Chocolate 10% Roast barley 10%	Pale 80% Chocolate or Crystal 12% Torrefied wheat 8%	Pale 80% Chocolate. 12% Roasted Barley 8%
Hops	Bittering – Fuggles Aroma – Fuggles	Fuggles	Bittering – Challenger Aroma – Goldings	Bittering – Challenger Aroma – Goldings
Other	Based on an 1880 Fuller's recipe	Add oyster essence during the boil if desired. Anchovies could be interesting instead.		Add up to 10% lactose at bottling
OG	1053	1048	1048	1048
IBU	33	33	30	30
Colour	140	200	75	75

Beer	Keighly Porter	Maclays Oat Malt Stout	Maclay Porter	Hog's Back Porter	Larkins Porter
Grain	Pale 85% Crystal 10% Chocolate 5%	Pale 70% Oat malt 22% Roast barley 6% Chocolate 2%	Pale 90% Wheat 5% Crystal 5%	Pale Malt 60% Crystal 20% Chocolate 20%	Pale 88% Crystal 7% Chocolate 5%
Hops	Bittering – East Kent and Styrian Goldings	Bittering – Fuggles	Bittering – Fuggles	Bittering – Goldings and Fuggles	Bittering – Goldings and Fuggles
Other		Compare this to historical recipe 27		Reduce the crystal malt if your batch is very dark.	Add the Fuggles 20 mins. before the end.
OG	1045	1045	1040	1046	1053
IBU	55	35	40	48	59
Colour	100	50	80	?	70

Anyone can finish the exercise for any beer. Will you get the exact copy? Rarely!

136

4.6 IF YOU REALLY WANT MORE LOOKALIKE STOUTS OR PORTER BEERS

- Buy Ray Daniels' *Designing Great Beers*. It was written for the US market so a little jiggery-pokery with units will be needed and it obviously has a US bent. They do brew great beers in the US so using this book could be a welcome broadening of horizons. I prefer any of the Graham Wheeler productions for CAMRA Books, such as *Brew Classic European Beers at Home*.
- Buy Roger Protz's *The Real Ale Almanac* (updated and published regularly by CAMRA).

You will brew some great beers. They may not be what you expect. Good luck.

Appendix One: History of Porter

Extract from The Art and Mystery of Brewing. Morrice 1802

HISTORY OF THE LONDON BREWERY

The Gentry, now, residing in London more than they had done in former Times, introduced the Pale Ale, and Pale Small Beer, which they were habituated to in the Country; and either engaged some of their Friends, or the London Brewers, to make for them' these Kinds of Drink ; and Affluence and Cleanliness promoted the delivery of them in the Brewer's own Casks, and at his Charge. Pale Malt being dearest, the Brewer, being loaded with more Tax and Expense, fixed the Price of such Small Beer at Eight Shillings and Ten Shillings per Barrel, and the Ale at Thirty Shillings per Barrel: the latter was sold by the Victualler at Fourpence per Quart, and under the Name of Twopenny.

This little Opposition excited the Brown Beer Trade to produce, if possible, a better Sort of Commodity, in their Way, than heretofore had been made. They began to Hop their Mild Beers more, and the Publican started three, four, or six Butts at a Time, but so little Idea had the Brewer, or his Customer, of being as the Charge of large Stocks of Beer, that it gave Room to a Set of monied People to make a Trade, by buying these Beers from Brewers, keeping them some Time, and selling them, when Stale, to Victuallers for Twenty-five Shillings or Twenty-six Shillings per Barrel.

Our Tastes but slowly alter or reform. Some drank Mild and Stale Beer; others, what was then called Three Threads, at Threepence per Quart; but many used all Stale, at Fourpence per Quart.

On this Footing stood the Trade until about the Year 1722; when the Brewers conceived that there was a Mean to be found preferable to any of these Extremes which was, that Beer should be well brewed and, from being kept its proper Time becoming Mellow (i.e. neither New nor Stale) it would recommend itself to the public. This they ventured to sell at Twenty-three shillings per Barrel that the Victualler might retail it at Three-pence per Quart.

Though it was slow, at first, in making its Way, yet, as it was certainly right in the End, the Experiment succeeded beyond Expectation, The labouring People, Porters, &c., sound its Utility; from whence came its Appellation of *Porter*, or *Entire Butt*. As yet, however, it was far from being in the Perfection which we have since had it.

Porter was, at different Times, raised to Thirty Shillings per Barrel, where it remained till the Year 1799, and was retailed at Threepence Halfpenny per Quart; when, in Consequence of Malt rising in Price to from Four Pounds to Four Pounds Ten Shilling's, and Five Pounds, per Quarter, and Hops from Four Pounds Ten Shillings to Seventeen Pounds, Eighteen Pounds, and Twenty Pounds per Hundred Weight, Porter was raised to Thirty-five Shillings per Barrel, and retailed at Fourpence per Quart. Ale, likewise, experienced a Rise of from Forty-two Shillings to Sixty-two Shillings and Sixpence per Barrel.

The Prices still keeping up, at a Meeting of the principal Porter Brewers it was raised to Forty Shillings per Barrel to the Victualler, and is retailed at Fourpence Halfpenny per Quart.

Appendix 2

Extract on Thermometers and Hydrometers from Philosophical Principles of the Science of Brewing. Richardson 1784

"The introduction of the thermometer into the practice of the brewery, general as it is now becoming, was by slow and cautious steps. The sturdy ignorance of a country fellow, dignified by the appellation of BREWER, too often opposed itself to the good sense and discernment of his employer, to the defeat of the intended improvement; though it did not always happen that this ignorance was unmixed with CUNNING. There was sometimes an apprehension that the instrument might become a rule in the master's hand, by which the abilities of the servant might be measured; and that the interference of the former might prove destructive of the importance of the latter.

"The prevalent practice of those days (and it is not yet annihilated) was whether to mix a given quantity of cold, to a given quantity of boiling water, in the copper, for the purpose of mashing; or to turn the boiling water into the mash tun and suffer it to remain until THE BREWER CAN SEE HIS FACE IN IT, before the malt were put into it; both of which were sufficiently ridiculous to be discontinued, where the means of measuring heat are to be obtained. As an appendage to this practice, the finger supplied the place of a thermometer, in determining the fermenting heat of the wort, and the brewer was persuaded that the delicacy of his sensations, in that business, precluded the necessity, and rendered impertinent the adoption of a substitute.

"Some of the brewers on the continent carry the matter still further, and determine the heat of the scalding liquor intended for mashing by the finger.

Since the first publication of these remarks the author has been credibly informed, that the first rudiments of the professional education of the greatest brewer in this kingdom, were founded on the principle here adduced. His hand was to be directed to be immersed in the liquor, and then make a short revolution in it. If he could bear only one or two of these revolutions, the liquor was too hot; but if he could accomplish THREE, it was in a proper state for mashing."

Of the saccharometer:

"The darkness in which the business of brewing in involved, extends even to the legislature itself, as is evinced by the frequent disputes between brewers and officers of excise, on the subject of distinguishing worts chargeable with the strong beer duty, from those which are to be charged only as small: and this seems to have occasioned the late act of parliament, for making separate and advanced charge upon table beer, to be compulsory to BREW IT ALONE; that the officer may not be puzzled in applying his only means of discrimination, consisting of dipping his finger into the wort, tasting it, etc. and from these instances it may be perceived that the finger is or has been a very important agent to both the brewer and to the revenue officer, in the exercise of their different functions. In this ignorance, also, originate those ridiculous restrictions which prohibit the mixing of small with strong beer in order to accommodate the palate of any person with the liquor he prefers.

"Were the duties charged according to the specific gravities of the wort, these altercations would immediately vanish, the revenue would be increased, the brewer would be at liberty to make, alter, or compound his liquor into as many and as various sorts as he had palates to please, without subjecting himself to the interference of the officer, or the lash of the law."

Monckton's editing. (*The History of English Ale and Beer*)

Appendix 3

Table of heats (for various malts) by Hayman. (Art of Brewing 1853)

Malt	1st Mash	2nd Mash
Very Pale	176°F	182°F
Pale and Amber mixed	172°F	178°F
High coloured amber	168°F	172°F
Equal portion of pale, amber and brown	160°F	166°F
All amber	170°F	176°F
Brown	155°F	164°F

Appendix 4

Extract from the Brown Malt production. The Maltsters Guide by Edward Skeate White (1860)

"During the operation of 'firing off the malt must not be left, as by a slight increase of heat beyond 180, it will scorch and be too high coloured. The operator examines the malt every' few minutes, and by the feel alone, knows when the process is finished, 'the hot malt at this time sends forth a peculiar sweet odour, which may be perceived at a great distance. The operation of firing, or finishing, should always be done with a very clear fire, or the ale will not fine. To pale ale brewers this is an important part of the process.

Amber malt is finished in a similar manner at a temperature of about 185 degrees, which has the effect of imparting to it a higher colour. When this kind is ground it is of a rich amber colour, hence its name. The fuel used for drying amber malt is different to that used for drying pale or ordinary. For the latter kinds the fire is made of anthracite coal or coke, but for the purpose of producing the true amber colour and its peculiar flavour, the fire is made of coal or coke, upon which is laid a few billets of wood, generally of oak. This has the effect not only of making a sharp fire in a short time, but also imparts the peculiar flavour supposed, to be derived from the pyroligneous acid thrown off during the combustion of the wood. Porter malt, which is used for the purpose of producing the dark, rich coloured beverage, known as Porter, is dried on the kiln in a very different manner to any of the former kinds. It is an operation which requires the greatest care; as, in consequence of the great heat employed, if neglected for a few moments towards the completion of the process, or if the heat be increased beyond a certain point, the malt would take lire. Indeed, with the utmost care, a sudden change of wind, or unexpected gust, will sometimes cause the hot malt to ignite, when the whole of it is destroyed. Such being the case, the best and steadiest of the workmen are selected as kiln-men, and receive more wages than the floor-men, or those whose duty it is to steep, couch, and turn the grain on the floor. Each kiln-man is attended by a boy, whose duty is to bring the wood and water. The floors of Porter malt kilns are mostly constructed of woven Stout wire, about a twentieth of an inch in diameter. The wire floor, or a floor of thin perforated iron plate is necessary for this purpose, as the fire must be raised and lowered in a few minutes, so as to produce a heat from 100 to a heat nearly approaching combustion. So rapid is the progress of drying Porter malt, that the operation does not occupy more than from one hour to one hour and a half. The fuel for this purpose should be of oak, elm, beech, birch, or hardwood faggots. When the grain is thrown on the kiln, it is carefully levelled, and does not exceed an inch and a half in depth. As the ordinary bars of the fire-place are too near the under part of the kiln floor, they are taken out and the fire made on the ground in the fire-place. Two small faggots are fired, upon which is laid some Stout wood. During the earlier part of the process it is requisite *(sic)* to keep the fire down a little, this is done by sprinkling on water from time to time. When the process is half finished, the fire is allowed to go out, and the doors and windows of the kiln opened for ten minutes to cool it. The malt is then carefully turned. The fire is then again made up and the doors and windows closed. After a few minutes, the heat is intense, the draught of air rushing over the burning faggots creates so sharp a fire, that the flame is carried nearly across to the opposite side of the under part of the kiln. The workman, by experience, knows to what extent the lire should be allowed to proceed, and regulates it by sprinkling water on the burning wood as previously observed. At this critical time, if the fire were not thus checked, the flame would increase so rapidly that it would soon communicate to the malt drying above, and set the whole in a blaze. When an accident of this kind happens, the flame shoots out from the top of the kiln several yards in height, similar to a jet of carburetted hydrogen gas from a gas main, accompanied by a humming noise resembling a deep toned organ, caused partly by the rush of air over the fire-place and up through the meshes of the wire flooring of the kiln. To prevent the fire extending to other parts of the malt-house, when the grain on the kiln ignites, some maltsters keep several iron buckets always filled with water close by the kiln door, so as to be ready to be discharged upon the burning grain.

A precaution like this should always be taken as when the fire first breaks out, it may soon be extinguished by a few buckets full of water if close at hand. During the latter part of the operation, the intense heat generates a quantity of steam in each grain, which by sudden expansion, explodes, bursting the husk with a loud .snap. From this circumstance the operation is termed "snapping" and the malt, " snapped malt." The explosion of the husk, attended by an expansion of the starch, causes a considerable enlargement of the grain, which is from twenty to twenty-five per cent above the dry barley. A bushel of this kind of malt weighs about 32 lbs.; as it has a blown or distended appearance, it is sometimes termed "blown malt", 'the principle object to be attained in the manufacture of Porter malt is the conversion of the sugar, gum, and starch, into a substance resembling the substance called caramel, which being a powerful colouring agent, imparts the peculiar brown colour to the beverage termed Porter. This substance possesses a peculiar grateful bitter flavour which is highly esteemed by many persons; in fact the taste of this bitter appears to become one of the strongest and most genera! of our methods of pleasing the palate. It equally recommends toast-water, and also the varieties of Brown Beer or Porter, in the preparation of which, malt is used in which the sugar. &e.. is partially caramelised by heat, as previously described. The caramel bitter is in fact a starch flavour, which we find modified by the most various accessories in different beverages, and even in solid varieties of food in a cooked state. The peculiar pleasing flavour of the well baked crust of bread owes its flavour to the partial caramelisation of the starch in the flour by the process of baking. In some diseases, Porter or Stout is recommended; this is also owing to the presence of caramel in the beverage, which is supposed to have a peculiar influence upon the system.

When Porter is brewed from malt, made in the manner previously described, it contains, in addition to the caramel bitter, a peculiar acidity. The hard wood faggots, used as fuel for drying the malt, contain an acid. known by the appellation of pyroligneous acid. The combustion of the wood liberates this acid, which being carried away by the strong draughts, passes through the wire flooring of the kiln, and penetrates the hot malt, which being more or less ruptured in the husk, is in a condition to be acted upon by the acid fume, which, seizing upon the exposed and partially caramelised starch, effects a combination with it. The acid is also formed in the grain itself in addition to that from the wood. When the malt is mashed, this acid is liberated and combines with the saccharine and dissolved caramel in the wort. In addition to the formation of pyroligneous acid, it is supposed that during the combustion of the wood, a certain amount of empyreumatic oil is also imparted to the malt drying on the kiln. Pyroligneous acid, derived from two words signifying fire and wood, is usually termed acetic acid by chymists. It is the acid of vinegar; in a concentrated form it has a very pungent and fragrant odour, when mixed with camphor and essential oil of spices it forms the aromatic vinegar used for vinaigrettes. It corrodes many metals; the acetate, or sugar of lead, is formed by dissolving in it the oxide of that metal, and with oxide of copper it produces verdigris. It is manufactured in large quantities in the neighbourhood of Swansea, by the destructive distillation of hard green wood. The green billets are put into a tight iron chamber, or retort, winch is heated by a strong fire, similar to the method of obtaining gas from coal. The vapour is condensed, which contains many impurities, such as, tar, wood naptha, and oil, which is separated by further distillation- the result is pure acetic acid. When well made, it has no peculiar smell or taste beyond that of pure acidity, as such is perfectly wholesome, and well adapted for pickling purposes. The impure, or, pyroligneous acid, containing tar, &c. possesses great preservative qualities. Meat or fish steeped in it for a short time will keep for an indefinite period, without the use of salt. Quebec oak contains great quantities of this acid, as may be perceived in the shavings of this wood, which is imported into this country and used for staves and cabinet work. If a handful of the newly planed shavings be held to the nose and breathed upon, the pungency of the acid is immediately detected.

The peculiar flavour of genuine unadulterated Porter and Stout, such as is brewed by the leading brewers in London, Dublin, and Cork is to be attributed to the method of drying the malt as alluded to, and cannot be introduced by any other process. This kind of malt is made expressly for these large firms. Small brewers sometimes attempt to brew Porter and Stout but as they do not use the true Porter malt, the effort is hopeless, the difference of flavour is soon detected.

The small brewer uses ordinary or pale malt, and makes up the deficient colour by using a small quantity of colouring matter, sometimes burnt sugar, but generally patent or roasted malt, this, it is true, may impart a burnt flavour and high colour, but not that peculiar flavour imparted by proper Porter malt. As the acid is also absent, it is sometimes counterfeited by introducing common epsom salts or sulphate of magnesia. There is also another kind of Porter malt, not quite so high coloured. It is not considered so well adapted for brewing Porter, and is generally used as a colouring agent. The kiln is constructed somewhat similar to that used for true Porter malt, but the floor instead of being square is circular."

Appendix 5

Making Brown Malt. London & Country Brewer. Ellis 1734

8   *The Nature of the* Barley-Corn,

CHAP. II.

Of making Malts.

AS I have described the Ground that returns the best Barley, I now come to treat of making it into Malt; to do which, the Barley is put into a leaden or tyled Cistern that holds five, ten or more Quarters, that is covered with water four or six Inches above the Barley to allow for its Swell; here it lyes five or six Tides as the Malster calls it, reckoning twelve Hours to the Tide, according as the Barley is in body or in dryness; for that which comes off Clays, or has been wash'd and damag'd by Rains, requires less time than the dryer Grain that was inned well and grew on Gravels or Chalks; the smooth plump Corn imbibing the water more kindly, when the lean and steely Barley will not so naturally; but to know when it is enough, is to take a Corn end-ways between the Fingers and gently crush it, and if it is in all parts mellow, and the husk opens or starts a little from the body of the Corn, then it is enough: The nicety of this is a material Point; for if it is infus'd too much, the sweetness of the Malt will be greatly taken off, and yield the less Spirit, and

146

fo will caufe deadnefs and fournefs in Ale or Beer in a fhort time, for the goodnefs of the Malt contributes much to the prefervation of all Ales and Beers. Then the water muft be drain'd from it very well, and it will come equal and better on the floor, which may be done in twelve or fixteen Hours in temperate weather, but in cold near thirty. From the Ciftern it is put into a fquare Hutch or Couch, where it muft lye thirty Hours for the Officer to take his Gage, who allows four Bufhels in the Score for the Swell in this or the Ciftern, then it muft be work'd Night and Day in one or two Heaps as the weather is cold or hot, and turn'd every four, fix or eight Hours, the outward part inwards and the bottom upwards, always keeping a clear floor that the Corn that lies next to it be not chill'd; and affoon as it begins to come or fpire, then turn it every three, four or five Hours, as was done before according to the temper of the Air, which greatly governs this management, and as it comes or works more, fo muft the Heap be fpreaded and thinned larger to cool it. Thus it may lye and be work'd on the floor in feveral Parallels, two or three Foot thick, ten or more Foot broad, and fourteen or more in length to Chip and Spire; but not too much nor too faft; and when it

Appendix 6

Durden Park Beer Circle Method of Creating Dark Malts

Some ingredients needed to make OLD BEERS might not be readily available, in particular pale amber, amber and brown malts. All three can be produced by roasting pale malt in an ordinary domestic oven as described below. Carapils with a colour number of about 25 can be used in place of pale amber up to 45% of the pale malt in any grist. Even carapils, however, might only be available by bulk purchase direct from maltsters.

ROASTING METHOD

Line a large baking tin with aluminium foil, and pour in pale malt to a depth of 12 mm (½ inch). Place in the oven (preferably fan-stirred) at 100°C (230°F) for 45 minutes to dry out the malt, then raise the temperature to 150°C (300°F). After a further 20 minutes remove 6 or 7 corns from the tray, slice across the centre with a sharp knife and compare the colour of the starchy centre with that of a few pale malt corns. The pale malt is almost pure white; for pale amber the colour should be the palest buff, just noticeably different from the pale malt. Continue heating until this colour is obtained, usually about 30 minutes.

For amber malt, continue heating until the cut section is distinctly light buff, usually 45 to 50 minutes. If brown malt is needed, raise the temperature at this point to 175°C (350°F) and wait until the cut cross-section is a full buff, i.e. about the colour of the paler types of brown wrapping paper. When the correct colour has been reached, remove the tray from the oven, allow to cool and store the roast grain in an air-tight screw-top jar (large kilner jars are ideal). If used soon after production, the flavour imparted by home-roasted grain is superior to bought grain.

The roasting times given above are intended only as a guide to producing the wanted roast grain Practical tests on the oven available will enable home-brewers to adjust the time and temperature to produce the colour needed.

Crystal malt, which is usually available, has about the same colour potential as brown malt but a more caramel-like flavour.

Appendix 7

Guinness Stout, Brewed for Mr. Amsinck and Recorded in his Log

56

No. 11. **DUBLIN STOUT.**—Gravity, 33 . 0, per Barrel.

March, Thursday, Atmosphere, 48 to 49 degrees.

Liquor, soft. No. 2 Analysis.

MALT.—New, Suffolk Pale, 29 at 336 lbs. per quarter.

Black 1⅞

Total ... 30⅞

HOPS.—New choice Yellow East Kent 424.

14 lbs. per quarter, 5¼ lbs. per barrel.

FIRST MASH.

		B. F. G.		
Heat in Tun,	168 degrees,	1 . 1 . 5	per quarter,	42 barrels.
„	Copper 175 „	0 . 2 . 4	„	18 „
	Total ...	2 . 0 . 0		60

Mashed ¾ hour, Stood 1 hour 10 minutes. Tap Heat 150 degrees.

SECOND MASH.

		B. F. G.		
Heat in Copper,	182 degrees,	0 . 1 . 3	per quarter,	10 barrels.
„	„ 182	0 . 2 . 0	„	15 „
	Total ...	0 . 3 . 3		25

Mashed, Stood ¾ hour. Tap Heat, 153 degrees.

Tap spent, and off, sparged at 187 degrees, 0 . 0 . 8 per quarter 7 barrels, stood ¼ hour, Tap Heat 153 degrees. Tap spent and off, sparged at 189 degrees, 0 . 0 . 8 per quarter, 7 barrels, stood 10 minutes, Tap Heat 150 degrees. Tap spent, and off, sparged at 196 degrees, 0 . 0 . 8 per quarter, 7 barrels, stood 10 minutes, Tap Heat 150 degrees. Tap spent, and off, sparged 201 degrees, 0 . 1 . 5 per quarter, 12 barrels, stood 10 minutes, Tap Heat 153 degrees. Tap spent, and off, sparged at 202 degrees, 0 . 1 . 3 per quarter, 10 barrels, Tap Heat 155 degrees.

Total liquor for the Gyle, 4 . 0 . 3 per quarter, 123 barrels.

RETURN WORT.

			B. F. G.		Bar.		
Sparged ...	at 190 degrees,		0.2.6	per quarter,	20 stood,	5 minutes.	
Do. (Tap off)	190	„	0.1.3	„	10 „	5	„
Do. do.	180	„	0.1.3	„	10 „	5	„
Do. do.	182	„	0.2.0	„	15 „	5	„
	Total		1.3.3		55		

This is the whole quantity of Return Wort, that could be made use of.

			B. F. G.		Bar.		
Sparged ...	at 182 degrees,		0.0.6	per quarter,	5 stood,	5 minutes.	
Do. (Tap off)	190	„	0.0.2	„	2 „	5	„
Do. do.	177	„	0.0.6	„	5 „	5	„
Mashed, cold			0.2.0	„	15 „	10	„
Do. do.			0.2.0	„	15 „	10	„
Sparged (Tap off) at 175		„	0.0.6	„	6 „	5	„
Do. do. cold			0.0.6	„	5 over Hops in Hop Back		
	Total		1.3.0		53		

This lot was thrown away, Mr. Guinness engaged to get 130 lbs. per quarter extract, therefore we went thus far, to give him a *chance* of doing so, which end of course he could not accomplish.

		B. F. G.			
Liquor turned over for the Gyle ...		4.0.3	per quarter	123 barrels.	
Do.	Return Wort	1.3.3	„	55	„
Do.	do.	1.3.0	„	53	„
	Total	7.2.6		231	

	Bar.			Bar.		Bar.
First Wort in Copper	39;	boiled, 1½ hour, out,	34;	wasted	5	
Second do.	80	„ 3 „	68	„	12	

First Wort in Square, 58 degrees, gauged, 25 barrels, 112 lbs. Yeast.
Second do. 58 „ „ 52 „ (3 a.m. Friday.)

I

Appendix 8

Porter Drinking in 1784

In his *Annals of the Royal Society Club* Sir Archibald Geikie FRS says that Faujas' description of this dinner is the only guest's view of the Royal Philosophers that we possess.

"About forty members of the Royal Society have been for more than twenty-five years, in the habit of dining together socially in one of the taverns of London. Each member has the right of bringing two guests, whom he chooses, among foreigners or friends of his own acquaintance in the Royal Society. The President may bring a greater number and may select whomever he pleases for guests.

We sat down to dinner about five o'clock. Sir Joseph Banks presided and filled the place of honour. No napkins were laid before us; indeed none were used; the dinner was truly in the English style. A member of the club who is a clergyman (I believe it was the astronomer Maskelyne) made a short prayer and blessed the company and the food. The dishes were of the solid kind, such as roast beef, boiled beef and mutton prepared in various ways, with abundance of potatoes and other vegetables, which each person seasoned as he pleased with the different sauces which were placed on the table in bottles of different shapes.

The beefsteaks and the roast beef were at first drenched with copious bumpers of strong beer, called Porter, drunk out of cylindrical pewter pots, which are much preferred to glasses because one can swallow a whole pint at a draught.

This prelude being finished, the cloth was removed and a handsome and well-polished table was covered, as if it were by magic, with a number of fine crystal decanters filled with the best port, Madeira and claret: this last is the wine of Bordeaux. Several glasses, as brilliant in lustre as fine in shape, were distributed to each person and the libations began on a grand scale, in the midst of different kinds of cheese, which, rolling in mahogany boxes from one end of the table to the other, provoked the thirst of the drinkers.

To give more liveliness to the scene, the President proposed the health of the Prince of Wales; this was his birthday; we then drank to the Elector Palatine, who was this day to be admitted into the Royal Society. The same compliment was next paid to us foreigners of whom there were five present. (Broussonet was one of them.)

The members of the Club afterwards saluted each other, one by one, with a glass of wine. According to their custom, one must drink as many times as there are guests, for it would be thought a want of politeness in England to drink to the health of more persons than one at a time.

A few bottles of champagne completed the enlivenment of every one. Tea came next, together with bread and butter and all the usual accompanyments: coffee followed, humbly yielding the preference to the tea, though it be the better of the two. In France we commonly drink only one cup of good coffee after dinner; in England they drink five or six of the most detestable kind.

Brandy, rum and some other strong liqueurs closed this philosophic banquet, which terminated at halfpast seven, as we had to be at a meeting of the Royal Society summoned for eight o'clock. Before we left, however, the names of all the guests were written on a large sheet of paper and each of us paid seven livres, four sols French money; this was not too dear. (It was about six shillings.)

I repaired to The Society along with Messrs Banks, Cavendish, Maskelyne, Aubert, and Sir Henry Englefield. We were all pretty much enlivened but our gaiety was decorous."

Appendix 9

Some Extracts and Colours of Modern Malts.

Kindly supplied by Fawcetts of Castleford.

Malt type	Characteristics	Extract	Colour
Marris Otter Pale	Well modified, producing consistent extract within the standard ale colour range, producing sweet and flavourful worts.	305	4.5-5.5
Caramalt	Very light and sweet malt flavour.	275	27-32
Crystal Malt	Toffee caramel flavour.	275	120-140
Dark crystal malt	Burnt coffee flavour. Adds ruby red colour to the beer.	275	200-400
Amber malt	Dry mild coffee flavour.	273	90-110
Brown malt	Dry mild coffee flavour.	273	140-160
Pale Chocolate Malt	Smooth coffee flavour.	273	500-550
Chocolate malt	Strong coffee flavour.	273	900-1000
Black malt	Very strong burnt coffee flavour.	273	1200-1400

Extract is measured in Litre degree/Kg.
Colour in EBC.

The above table reveals that roasted malts provide more extract than one may have supposed. The brewer's problem was that much of it wasn't fermentable.

Appendix 10

Amsinck Water Analyses

Amsinck is a rare treat and normally provides exact details of his brewing liquors. The numbers given refer to the water analysis quoted in a brewing method in this book. Amsinck always played down the importance of water, claiming the skill of the brewer was much more relevant.

No.1

Component	Quantity grains/imp. gal. (ppm)	Comment
CO_3^{2-} from Ca	6.18 (7.7)	Very good Brown Beer or Old Ale, but not for mild or running ales.
$CaSO_4$	11.68 (14.6)	
Organic		
$MgCl_2$		
$FePO_4$	0.24 (0.3)	
$MgSO_4$	25.6 (32)	
$MgCO_3$	1.08 (1.35)	
Na_2SO_4	24.25 (30.3)	
Na_2CO_3		
K_2CO_3		
NaCl	12.74 (15.9)	
Silicic acid	0.44 (0.6)	

No. 2

Component	Quantity grains/imp. gal. (ppm)	Comment
CO_3^{2-} from Ca		Very soft. Good for Brown Beers and Old Ales made from Hertfordshire malt. Not good for mild or running ales.
$CaSO_4$	1.01 (1.25)	
Organic		
$MgCl_2$		
$FePO_4$		
$MgSO_4$		
$MgCO_3$		
Na_2SO_4	1.88 (2.35)	
Na_2CO_3		
K_2CO_3	1.95 (2.4)	
NaCl	2.33 (2.9)	
Silicic acid		

No.8

Component	Quantity grains/imp. gal. (ppm)	Comment
CO_3^{2-} from Ca	19.75 (24.7)	"I have tasted as fine Ale brewed from this liquor as it is possible to produce but there is too much carbonate of lime for economy of hops".
$CaSO_4$	5.36 (6.7)	
Organic		
$MgCl_2$	1.63 (2.0)	
$FePO_4$		
$MgSO_4$		
$MgCO_3$		
Na_2SO_4		
Na_2CO_3		
K_2CO_3		
NaCl	1.39 (1.7)	
Silicic acid		

Appendix 11

Amsinck's Thoughts on Brown Beer Brewing Around 1860

BROWN BEER BREWED IN SEASON – Stout 30 lbs. gravity, 160 Degrees in tun, Tap Heat 144 to 145 Degrees, Porter 21 lbs. gravity, 157 Degrees in tun, Tap Heat 140 to 142 Degrees, in *summer* 3 Degrees lower.

These heats are for Hard Liquor, Soft required less by two degrees in the Tap Heat.

Underback should be covered close, before setting the tap, and if for convenience, you are obliged to keep it there for a time, it is good to have a coil of pipe to blow steam through, to advance the heat of the wort before going into the Copper or boiling back, if you can pump at once into the copper, do so,and cover over, lose no heat anywhere prior to the wort boiling, as soon as the Hops are in, and the wort boiling keep it so *vigorously* for the time you propose.

SPARGING – There are various modes of conducting this operation, Brewers as in other parts of the process of brewing differ widely; I have tried all, first take the original Scotch System, after you have completed the mash, sufficient time before setting tap, sparge to get the tun full, and after setting tap, continue sparging, until the intended quantity of liquor for the gyle is exhausted, by this method the goods never dry, this plan I do not approve of.

I prefer allowing the wort from the first mash to be quite spent, then have the goods levelled over the tun, turn the tap *off* and sparge on half the quantity determined upon, to make up the first copper of wort, allow it to remain twenty minutes, then set tap and sparge on the remaining half gently, the object in turning *off* the tap, the first half is, that the liquor may percolate evenly, over the whole surface, and raise the goods off the bottom, then the remaining half of the liquor washes every grain.

You will observe in the example that I prefer two mashes, and two sparges, my practice in detail is fully explained in the brewings.

The Dublin Brewers, at least as far as my practical experience is derived, prefer a rinsing process, a Mr. Guinness who was represented, to be a nephew of the great person of that name in the trade, gave me a day's brewing for their fine Stout, which you will find under the head of Dublin Stout, the process is slow, but more Extract produced with the quantity of liquor turned over, than I have seen in any other method.

COOLING – Here again there is no need of controversy, on the method of cooling, whether it is better to have no cooler or to have coolers, that is the question, who is to decide positively; some commence refrigerating directly, some at 160 degrees, at 120 degrees, and at 90 degrees. My opinion I that all are equally good, as far as the wort is concerned, some take the wort direct from the Hop Back, through the Refrigerator, and have been made on this head, have afterwards changed their opinion, and gone to coolers again.

Brewers who have not had much practice, and consequently have no confidence in themselves, or I should say in the principles of brewing, fear that the wort will become acidified by exposure to the air, now as long as the heat of the Wort is higher than that of the Atmosphere, no bad effect on the wort can be produced, and as it is *always* higher of course there can be no harm in exposure to the atmosphere.

FERMENTATION – Pitching is an important part, as far as the Yeast is concerned, the Yeast from a Gyle brewed on Monday, and cleansed or skimmed on the Wednesday would be in condition for pitching on Saturday or Monday following, and no longer, and in summer stop at Saturday, drain off thebeer as solid as possible, or what is better pressed through Needham and Kite's Filter Press, on the *same* day, that it is intended to be made use of, the wort should be pitched at the same heat as you intend the Gyle to be, when altogether in the Tun, after a few barrels, say three or four inches of wort covering the bottomof the tun, put the yeast in, and have it well swept about, and mixed with the wort, roused occasionally, until all the wort is down.

I am a firm advocate for rousing, Light Ale commence 24 hours after pitching, until within 12 hours of skimming, or cleansing, Strong Ale 36 hours after pitching, until within 12 hours of skimming or cleansing.

With regard to attenuation, the best rule is to cleanse or skim, when half way from the original gravity, for Ale I prefer 70 degrees for a maximum heat, the gyle should be allowed to attain.

Stout and Porter, the same rule in attenuation, up to a heat of 75 or 80 degrees.

The majority of Country Brewers, are in favour of attenuating , as low as possible, that is as low s they can get it, 30 lbs. gravity worked down to 7 or 8 lbs. I prefer when clean for sale to find it 12 or 13 lbs., you then get a rich, fine flavoured Ale.

Appendix 12

Brewing log for a Porter Beer around 1860

154

The following statement was instituted by me, for my own satisfaction, as well as that of my employer, and was handed to him quarterly, it was much valued, the proof of its correctness was founded on the Stock books. Every quarter of Malt, every pound of Hops, every barrel of Beer, was accounted for. Stock of Beer was taken every night.

PORTER.—First day of April, to the last day of June, inclusive.

		Qrs.	
MALT.—Old Pale	... ...	280	61s.
New do.	... ...	520⅝	61s.
New Brown	... ...	249	54s.
Black	...	37⅜	58s.

	£ s. d.
Total 1087	3022 11 10

Return Wort from **X, XX, XXX, $\frac{K}{XXXX}$ S** equal

Bar. Lbs. T.	s. d.	
to 212½ at 21 . 0	14 4	142 6 0

	Total ...	3164 17 10	p.bar.13 1¾

Bar. Lbs. T.
Return Wort to S equal to 13 at 21 . 0 ... ... 14 4   9 6 4 | 3155 11 6

Hops, Planter.	Growth.	Bas.	Pos.	Cloth.	Hops.	Total.	Price.			
				Lbs.	Lbs.	Lbs.	s.			
Hunt	1840	,,	2	10	247	257	252	28	18	0
Brittenden	,,	,,	3	15	383	398	137/6	24	9	0
Shoobridge	1839	,,	9	45	1700	1745	62	48	5	0
Larkin	,,	1	,,	25	388	413	70	12	18	2
Murton	,,	,,	2	10	198	208	105	9	15	0
Peale	1838	2	,,	50	360	410	112	20	10	0
Sharpe	,,	,,	19	95	2775	2170	50	64	1	3
Parish, Gibbons	,,	,,	25	125	4192	4387	105	202	7	2
Pressed Bags ...	Old.	2	,,	50	574	624	94	26	3	6
Total		5	60	425	10817	11242		(9¼d. per lb.)	437 7 1	

	£ 3592 18 7

Lbs. T. Lbs. T.
Gravity 21 . 0 per barrel Extract 90 . 0 per quarter

	Bar. B. F. G.	ʄ £ s. d.
Length	4798—4 . 1 . 5¾ per quarter, Cost per barrel	0 14 11½
Racked	4611—4 . 0 . 8¾ ,, ,, ,,	0 15 6¾

Extract 8¾d. per pound.

Not the Last Word

When is a book finished? Never! At the last minute we find the thing for which we may have been searching all along – and then again it is perhaps just another irrelevancy in the vast collection of material on stout and porter, that I have collected.

But I can't restrain myself. So try this out.

Harwood, allegedly, called his mixture of beers, a pot 'o three threads. (Bickerdyke).

Sometime within the next thirty years this came to be known as porter. (Ellis)

Why?

The market labourers?

The take away deliverers?

There is no evidence of a convincing nature for any of these theories but I do like the idea that the name porter may be a play on words and may be Scottish in origin, not from London!

I hear the groans of disbelief, but Gwen Enstam, Assistant Editor of the SLDL tells me that the Scottish National Dictionary says of the word "porter":

"Weaving usage: A section of the reed in a loom containing 20 interstices through which the warp threads are passed, the width of the interstice being determined by the number of these contained in an "ell" of 37 inches and therefore in turn determining the density of the weave, called in Eng. "a beer"."

It is a derivative of the (now obsolete) English word "port", meaning to carry, sc. the warp threads.

The dates in the SND for the usage of "porter" are up to 1930. "

So.....pot 'o three threads.......weaving.......Scottish word porter describes the holder of the warp threads in weaving terminology...... ..and determines the weave density....... i.e the number of threads...... .called beer in English.

So maybe some Scottish imbibers took the pot 'o three threads name and played upon it one dark wet Scottish night as the peat hissed in the open grate and they drank some mixture along with a dram no doubt. Why not? There is no evidence the name has its origin in London.

Time for more research I think.

Brewing Terms

Acetification :- Turn to vinegar. Some bacteria can continue to oxidise ethanol to ethanoic acid, formerly called acetic acid, commonly called vinegar.

Acidity:- See pH.

Alkalinity :- Some salts have the ability to alter the pH of water. Calcium hydrogen carbonate $(Ca(HCO_3)_2)$ lifts the value above 7 (neutral) and is said to increase alkalinity.

Alpha acids :- Bittering compounds in hops.

Ambient temperature :- Temperature of the surroundings.

Amsinck :- Victorian Brewmaster, who recorded brews he did or was present at, faithfully.

Anaerobic :- Without oxygen, as applied to a yeast working in a fermentation.

Aeration:- Getting air into solution, in order to provide oxygen for aerobic fermentation. Nowadays effected with a pump and sterile filter or gas washer. See rousing.

Aerobic :- With oxygen, as applied to a yeast working in a fermentation.

Attenuate :- Convert the fermentable sugar to alcohol.

Back :- From buck or bucket. Any holder of liquid; e.g. Underback = container on the floor.

Barley :- The grain from which most European and US beers are made.

Beer styles :- The opinions of a self appointed few, who try to tell the rest of us, what a beer should be like; e.g. this book.

Blown malt:- 19th century malt made by vigorously heating green malt, causing it to swell.

Bottom mashing :- Running the mash liquor in from underneath the goods.

Brewer:- Man who brews beer.

Brewster:- Woman who brews beer.

Brown malt:- 18th century malt, made by heating partially dried or wet green malt to give it colour. See blown malt.

Burton :- Town in Middle England, famed for its pale ales and bitters, due to the high calcium sulphate content in the water.

Bushel:- Volume of malt, around 8 gallons.

$CaCO_3$:- Chemical formula for calcium carbonate, which is formed when calcium hydrogen carbonate decomposes during boiling or brewing. If it is not removed prior to brewing, it may detrimentally affect the beer and mash efficiency. Many brewers choose to ignore its effects.

Caramelisation :- Decomposing sugars by removing hydrogen and oxygen atoms, leaving carbon. Hence the darker colour of caramel.

Cask hops:- Hops added to the cask in which the beer is maturing or
     conditioning. Also called dry hopping. They may nowadays
     be added during the primary or secondary fermentation and
     still be called cask hops, but shouldn't be. Cask hops provide
     aromatic oils without increasing the bittering substantially. See
     copper hopping.

Casking :- Filling beer into a cask or keg, usually in order to leave
     some solids behind as sediment and to preserve the beer.

Cleansing :- Scottish brewing term for racking off after fermentation
     and letting the yeast settle for a few days before further racking.

Cold break:- As the wort cools suspended and dissolved particles settle
     out to leave a clear wort. Called the cold break. (See hot break)

Copper :- Any vessel used for boiling or heating a liquid. Formerly
     often made from copper.

Copper hops:- Hops used to supply bittering, by boiling with the wort.

Courage:- London Brewery, founded in the 19th century.

Craft Brewers:-Home brewers who brew according to the brewing
     craft-rather than use easy-use kits of, mainly, dubious pedigree
     – as exemplified by the "Craft Brewing Association" the UK's
     home brewing organisation.

Diastatic power:- The ability of the enzymes in malt to convert starch
     and higher sugars into maltose and other fermentable matter.

Dickens Charles:- Victorian writer, active in London, and famous for
     his social comment and record of Victorian life and habits.

Dry hop:- See cask hops

Durden Park Beer Circle:- Home Brewing Club in West London
     famous for their work on researching forgotten beers and
     Praised by Michael Jackson as "Brewing Archeologists." They
     have tracked down and researched old brewing records for over
     20 years and their final version of 'Old British Beers and How
     to Brew Them' will be published soon).

EBC :- Method of assigning a number to help identify the colour
     (darkness) of a beer. The higher the number, the darker the
     beer.

Entire Butts (buts):- Original name given by Harwood tot eh drink,
     which came to be known as Porter.

Enzymes :- Molecules capable of breaking down large starch or sugar
     molecules into fermentable maltose. Their effectiveness is
     controlled by temperature and pH. In beer brewing they are
     the diastase enzymes, which are again divided into two types,
     alpha and beta, depending on the temperature and pH at which
     they best work. The protease are also important in brewing, as
     they break down sticky heavy protein molecules in poor quality

malt. Enzymes are also called biological catalysts. They are essential in driving the chemical processes in all living things.

Export:- A beer strong enough in alcohol and bitter enough in hops to withstand the rigours of a long sea journey.

Extraction:- The amount of material converted into soluble compounds and removed from the malt. The extract is the wort.

Farnham:- Area near the town of that name on the Surrey Hampshire border, famous for its hops, which are no longer available under that name.

Fermentable :- Any sugar capable of being turned to alcohol by yeast.

FG:- Final gravity. Also called racking gravity. The density of the young beer, prior to being racked into casks for the last time. The material responsible for the FG being greater than 1.000 is used in the secondary fermentation and is responsible for conditioning.

Foxed:- Description of beer, which has undergone unwanted bacterial attack. (supposed to make it smell like a fox). Sometimes referred to as "blinked".

Fuggles :- British hop, commonly used in IPAs and Porters and Stouts and still available.

Goldings:- British hop, commonly used in IPAs and Porters and Stouts and still available.

Goods :- The material (grist) in the mash tun.

Gravity :- Correct name is specific gravity. The density of a wort, divided by the density of water and expressed without the decimal point. E.g. 1050 is a wort of density $1.050g/cm^3$

Green malt:- Barley is allowed to germinate and then dried to form malt. The germinated but not yet dried barley is called green malt.

Grist:- Any cereal used to make beer, usually malted barley.

Grits :- Any cereal used as an additional starch source to malted barley, usually because it is much cheaper than malt, or because the malt nitrogen content is too high and low nitrogen grits artificially lower said figure. Also called adjuncts.

Gyle :- Nowadays usually taken to mean "a brew". Actually it meant the total volume of wort available for fermentation.

Gypsum :- Calcium Sulphate. See Burton.

HCO_3^- :- Hydrogen carbonate ion, almost always present in natural water as calcium hydrogen carbonate. This ion is unstable when heated and precipitates out as chalk, (calcium carbonate).

Hogshead:- Measure of beer volume, usually 54 gallons.

Hops :- Dried female flowers of the climber Humulus lupulus. Used in beer since the 17th century for flavouring and for their preservative qualities.

Hot break:- Suspended particles in the wort collide and coagulate during boiling. They become big enough to settle out and the wort clears. This point is called the hot break. (See cold break)

Hygroscopic:- Many materials, including malt, have a great affinity for water. They are able to take water from the air and raise their own moisture level. This often leads to foodstuffs being quickly ruined. (See slack malt)

IBU :- Method of assigning a number to help identify the bittering (as supplied by hops) of a beer. The higher the number, the more bitter the beer.

India IPA:- An export ale, sent to India and other destinations and also enjoyed in Britain. The modern beer is much weaker and lower in flavour than the 19th century version.

Isomerisation:- Changing the shape of a molecule, without altering the ratio of the atoms. The isomerised molecule may or may not have the same/similar properties to the precursor. In brewing the alpha acids present in the hop flower are isomerised by boiling and this increases their bittering properties.

Kedgeree :- Indian dish, excellent with IPA.

Keeping beers:- Beers strong enough or bitter enough to resist bacterial infection and so keep a long time. See Export.

Kive: Irish word for mash tun.

L. s. d.:- Pounds, shillings and pence. The old non-decimal currency of the UK. The price per barrel sometimes in pounds, but more usually in shillings, was used to name a beer. E.g. sixty shilling beer, written 60/-.

Lactobacilli :- Bacteria able to convert sugars into lactic acid (sour milk). It is essential to protect the wort or young beer from lactobacilli. The high alcohol concentrations and hopping rates inhibit lactobacilli growth in IPA. They are effectively destroyed by dilute bleach solution, but will reappear (always).

Malt :- Cereal, usually barley, which has been germinated so that energy food converting enzymes are released, and then dried so that the enzymes are dormant and preserved for the brewer. The enzymes are reactivated by the mash.

March:- Latest winter month (n the Northern Hemisphere) in which beer should traditionally be brewed.

Mashing :- Stirring malt with water to activate the enzymes and convert starch to fermentable maltose sugar.

McCrorie James:- Member of Durden Park and an authority on historical Scottish Beers, especially IPA and Majority Ales. Founder of the Craft Brewing Association, the UK's homebrewing organisation.

October:- Earliest winter month (in the Northern Hemisphere) in which beer should traditionally be brewed.

OG :- (Original Gravity) See also Starting gravity. The gravity of a wort before pitching with yeast.

Pale malts:- Malt which has been carefully dried and hardly roasted, in order to preserve its pale colour and high enzyme activity. The palest modern malts are lager malt and in the 19th century, was white malt.

pH:- Hydrogen ion concentration expressed logarithmically. A measure of acidity or alkalinity, usually on a scale from 0-14. 0-6 is acidic, 7 is neutral, and 8-14 alkaline. For brewing purposes the pH of mash liquor should be 7-8 and during a mash and fermentation should fall to acidic, in the range 4.5-5.5. Brewers purchase narrow range (4-8) pH indicator papers. pH meters measure the hydrogen ion concentration directly but need a lot of TLC in order to work accurately. pH papers are probably a better buy for small brewers of pale ales. But even they, cheap as they are, are much of a waste of time, especially for darker worts, and especially as a good mash liquor and good malt always manage to hit the right pH for enzyme activity.

Pitch :- Add working yeast to a wort to ferment it.

Primary fermentation:- The most vigorous part of a fermentation, during which the maltose is converted to alcohol and carbon dioxide.

Pyrolisis:- Heating an organic molecule until only the carbon is left. Burning food.

Rack:- Transfer from one vessel to another, usually with a view to leaving a sediment behind and preserving the beer or wort.

Rouse :- Stir to occlude oxygen and/or to keep the yeast working by preventing it settling or rising and becoming unavailable for fermentation.

Run off:- The first or second worts or the sparge liquor are removed from the goods by "running off."

Second mash :- Washing the maltose solution from the goods, by running a fresh liquor charge onto the goods and infusing. Actually not a mash at all, but a wash process. Historically it was called mash out of ignorance. (See sparging).

Secondary Fermentation:- A much slower fermentation of higher sugars to produce a variety of taste components. This takes place in a cask or bottle. It is referred to as maturation or conditioning.

SG:- Starting Gravity. See OG. Can also stand for specific gravity, depending on the context.

Set tap:- Run the wort off the grist.

Shive:- To put a bung into a cask. See spile.

Skimming :- Skimming the yeast head off a fermenting brew.

Slack(ed):- Scottish term. To set the tap, i.e. to run the wort off the grist.

164

Slack malt:- Malt which has been allowed to take up water from the air after drying. (See hygroscopic)

Sodium metabisulphite :- Powerful sterilising agent. Decomposes to form sulphur dioxide gas, which will destroy enzyme activity in beer but can be useful outside the cask.

Sparge :- Running water through the goods, to extract the maltose solution, called wort. See second mash.

Spile:- Thin weak cask plugs, functioned as a safety valve. They are only noted when they were "not porous." This would indicate high attenuation before casking, i.e. the young beer was well flat and not much carbon dioxide was still to be expected. A porous spile allowed gas exchange. See shive.

Stitch:- A Brown Beer, brewed a little weaker than Stout beers

Strike temperatures :- Temperature at which the grist is added to the mash liquor or vice versa.

Store:- Scottish word for a working active yeast.

Tap temperature :- Originally the temperature of the wort running out the tap. May be interpreted as the mash temperature when thinking modern day.

Torrefied :- Rude treatment of cereals, rendering them only fit for colouring and flavour, but not for extract.

Turning under, turning over :- See bottom mashing.

Ushers:- Famous Scottish brewery, celebrated for the quality of its beers. An English brewery of the same name also brewed some fine beers

Victorian :- Adjective to describe things taking place during the reign of Queen Victoria, (1837-1901). Now taken to mean the last 60-70 years of the 19th century.

Vineous:- Description of beer if the alcohol has been allowed to oxidise to sugar.

v/v:- Volume of alcohol in a given volume of beer. Usually expressed as a percentage.

w/v:- Weight of alcohol in a given volume of beer. Usually expressed as a percentage.

w/w:- Weight of alcohol in a given weight of beer. Usually expressed as a percentage. For all intents and purposes the same as w/v, the density of beer being practically $1.000g/cm^3$.

Yeast :- Micro-organism capable of converting sugars to alcohol and carbon dioxide.

Young beer :- Freshly fermented beer after the primary fermentation, but not conditioned. See secondary fermentation

Younger's :- Famous Edinburgh brewery

Bibliography

Literature used in this work or useful for further research.

Amsinck G.S. *Practical Brewing.* London 1868

Bickerdyke John. *The Curiosities of Ale & Beer.* 1889

Black William *A Practical Treatise on Brewing, and on storing of beer, etc.* Smith, Elder & Co.: London 1835

Booth D *Art of Brewing* London 1852

Brewer The Loftus London 1863

Child Samuel *Every Man his own Brewer. A small treatise, explaining the art and mystery of brewing Porter, ale, etc.* London 1790

Combrune Michael *An Essay on Brewing. With a view of establishing the principles of the art.*
London 1758

Combrune Michael *The Theory and Practice of Brewing* London 1762

Cook James *Selections from his Journals* Dover Publications New York 1971

Defoe Daniel. *Moll Flanders* Penguin Books

Ellis William *The London and country brewer* London 1736 & 1760

Fielding Henry. *Tom Jones.* Penguin Books 1997. (First published 1747)

Harrison J. An introduction to old British Beers and how to make them. Durden Park Beer Club. 1991

Hart-Davis Adam *What the Victorians Did for Us* Headline Book Publishing, London 2001

Hilton Timothy *The Pre-Raphaelites* Thames & Hudson London 1970

Hornsey Ian, *Brewing* RSC Cambridge 1999

Hough Richard, *Captain James Cook*, Hodder and Stoughton London 1995

Korzonas Al, *Homebrewing Volume 1* Sheaf & Vine Illinois 1997

Lane Maggie, *Jane Austen and Food,* Hambledon Press, London 1995

La Pensée Clive & Protz Roger *India Pale Ales* CAMRA Books 2001

La Pensée Clive *The Historical Companion to House-Brewing.* Kings England 2003

La Pensée Clive, *The Craft of House-Brewing,* Montag Publications 1996

Mann Thomas *Der Zauberberg* Fischer Verlag Berlin 1924

Mathias Peter *The Brewing Industry in England 1700-1830.* Cambridge University Press 1959

Milton Giles *Nathaniel's Nutmeg* Hodder & Stoughton 1999

Monckton H.A. *A History of English Ale & Beer* The Bodley Head Ltd. London 1966

Morrice Alexander *A Treatise on Brewing: wherein is exhibited the whole process of ... brewing* Symonds: London 1802

Mortimer. J *The Art of Husbandry* London 1712

O'Brian Patrick, *Joseph Banks* Harvill Press London 1997

Plumb J.H. *England in the Eighteenth Century* Pelican Books London 1963

Protz Roger, *Classic Stout & Porter* Prion London 1997

Protz Roger, *The Real Ale Almanac 5th Edition* CAMRA Books Glasgow 1997

Richardson John *Science of Brewing* London 1798

Richardson John *Philosophical Principles of the Science of Brewing* London 1784

Roberts W.H. *The Scottish Ale Brewer* Oliver & Boyd. Edinburgh 1838

Sambrook Pamela, *County House Brewing in England 1500-1900* Hambledon Press 1996

Skeate-White.E. *The Matster's Guide* 1860

Stopes. S.*Malt and Malting* F.W.Lyon: London 1885

Strong. L.A.G. *A Brewer's Progress 1757-1957*; Privately printed by Charrington's Brewery 1957

Tolstoy. Leo *The Kreutzer Sonata and other Stories* OUP 1998

Tuck. John *The Private Brewer's guide to the art of brewing ale and Porter, etc.* W. Simpkin and R. Marshall: London 1822

Watkins George *The Complete English Brewer; or, the Whole art and mystery of brewing, etc.* London 1773

Whitebrook William *The Art and Mystery of Brewing, laid open to every family* London 1822

Index

RECIPES

CAMRA Books

Buy more home-brewing books directly from CAMRA.

BUYING IN THE UK

All our books are available through bookshops in the UK. If you can't find a book, simply order it from your bookshop using the ISBN number, title and author details given below. CAMRA members should refer to their regular monthly newspaper What's Brewing for the latest details and member special offers. CAMRA books are also available by mail-order (postage free) from: CAMRA Books, 230 Hatfield Road, St Albans, Herts, AL1 4LW. Cheques made payable to CAMRA Ltd. Telephone your credit card order on 01727 867201. Also via the web site www.camra.org.uk

Carriage of £3.00 per book (Europe) and £6.00 per book (US, Australia, New Zealand and other overseas) is charged.

HOMEBREW CLASSICS – IPA

by Clive La Pensee and Roger Protz
196 pages   Price: £8.99
ISBN 1-85249-129-9

The Homebrew Classics series tells you everything you need to know about IPA. You will discover the history behind the beer, the characters and economic and social history behind the scene. The book also provides the background knowledge about ingredients and technique so that you can can reproduce the style authentically with your homebrew equipment.

BREW YOUR OWN REAL ALE AT HOME

by Graham Wheeler and Roger Protz
196 pages   Price: £8.99
ISBN 1-85249-138-8

This book contains recipes which allow you to replicate some famous cask-conditioned beers at home or to customise brews to your own particular taste. Conversion details are given so that the measurements can be used world-wide.

BREW CLASSIC EUROPEAN BEERS AT HOME

by Graham Wheeler and Roger Protz
196 pages   Price: £8.99
ISBN 1-85249-117-5

Keen home brewers can now recreate some of the world's classic beers. In your own home you can brew superb pale ales, milds, Porters, Stouts, Pilsners, Alt, Kolsch, Trappist, wheat beers, sour beers, even the astonishing fruit lambics of Belgium… and many more. Measurements are given in UK, US and European units, emphasising the truly international scope of the beer styles within.

HOME BREWING

by Graham Wheeler
240 pages   Price: £8.99
ISBN 1-85249-137-X

Recently redesigned to make it even easier to use, this is the classic first book for all home-brewers. While being truly comprehensive, Home Brewing also manages to be a practical guide which can be followed step by step as you try your first brews. Plenty of recipes for beginners and hints and tips from the world's most revered home brewer.

DICTIONARY OF BEER

By CAMRA
208 pages   Price: £7.99
ISBN 1-85249-158-2

A unique reference work. Where else would you find definitions of the following words grouped together: parachute, Paradise, paraflow and paralytic? Or skull-dragged, slummage and snob screen? More than 2000 detailed definitions. This dictionary covers brewing techniques and ingredients; international beers and breweries; tasting (beer evaluation) terms; historical references and organisations; British real ale breweries; slang phrases and abbreviations; culinary terms and beer cocktails; and much more.

50 GREAT PUB CRAWLS

by Barrie Pepper
256 pages   Price: £9.99
ISBN 1-85249-142-6

Visit the beer trails of the UK, from town centre walks, to hikes and bikes and a crawl on a train on which the pubs are even situated on your side of the track! Barrie Pepper, with contributions and recommendations from CAMRA branches, has compiled a 'must do' list of pub crawls, with easy to use colour maps to guide you, notes on architecture, history and brewing tradition to entertain you.

CAMRA'S GOOD CIDER GUIDE

by David Matthews
400 pages   Price: £9.99
ISBN 1-85249-143-4

CAMRA's guide to real cider researched anew CAMRA's guide to real cider and now with features on cider around the world. The guide contains features on cider-making, a comprehensive and detailed guide to UK producers of cider and a brand new listing of outlets – pubs, restaurants, bars, small cider makers – with full address including postcode and telephone contact numbers. Also provided are details o ciders available and, where appropriate, item of interest in the pub or area.

CAMRA'S LONDON PUBS GUIDE

by Lynne Pearce
256 pages   Price: £9.99
ISBN 1-85249-164-7

Real ale and great food in London pubs wit stories to tell. What could be better? This i your guide to finding excellent real ale in th capital. The book provides detailed descrip tions of CAMRA's top 250 London pubs together with street level maps and a selectio of illustrations.

Pubs are listed with opening times, trave details, food arrangements, parking, disable and children's facilities indicated. Plus the all important range of beers.

GOOD BOTTLED BEER GUIDE

By Jeff Evans
224 pages   Price: £8.99
ISBN 1-85249-173-6

The definitive guide to real ale in a bottle:
• all UK breweries which produce bottle-con ditioned beer
• tasting notes to help you choose carefully
• the background to each beer
• where the beer is on sale
• key dates in bottled beer history
• how to buy, keep and serve bottled real ale
• the best foreign bottle-conditioned beers

Highly commended by the British Guild o Beer Writers, this book has the answers fo those who like the idea of trying some of th most creatively brewed beers in the world There are more than 300 to choose from, a from the comfort of your armchair!

REAL ALE ALMANAC

By Roger Protz
320 pages   Price: £8.99
ISBN   1-85249-170-1

The Almanac is unique among beer books in listing every cask-conditioned beer brewed in Britain. This new edition lists brewpubs as well as commercial breweries. The Almanac also gives full details of the ingredients used for each beer – malts and hops in particular – along with author Roger Protz's own tasting notes based on a quarter-century experience of the brewing industry. The Almanac also indicates which beers are organic and those which are suitable for vegetarians and vegans.

PUBS FOR FAMILIES

By Adrian Tierney-Jones
256 pages   Price: £12.99
ISBN 1-85249-183-3

CAMRA's guide to pubs suitable for families lists those traditional pubs with real ale which also cater for children – from toddlers to teenagers.

This book lists the specialist features parents want to know about, such as childrens' organised games, suitable food choices, play equipment, nappy-changing facilities, garden area etc.

Adrian Tierney-Jones is a well-known food and drink writer with a young family of his own. He is tireless in the task of seeking out family-friendly pubs.

ROOM AT THE INN

By Tim Hampson
256 pages   Price: £12.99
ISBN 1-85249-184-1

Room at the Inn is a unique guide to quality overnight accommodation in real ale pubs.

The guide has been surveyed and researched from scratch for the third edition.

Each entry in the guide gives directions, contact details, opening times, type and extent of accommodation, list of beers, meal types and times, and an easy to understand price guide.

There are also snippets about local attractions and the sometimes centuries-old tales associated with the pub.

Whether on holiday or business, this is the only B&B guide for real ale fans.

CAMRA's Light And Dark Supporters committee campaigns to save all beers that are light in strength and all beers that are dark in colour.

These beers include Stouts, Porters and Old Ales as well as Light and Dark Milds, 60/- Ales and Low Gravity Bitters (those with an ABV of 3.4% or less). So are all these styles of beer under threat of extinction? No, in fact some are actually growing in popularity, but all are much more difficult to find in cask conditioned form than the bitters that you normally see on handpump when you walk into a pub.

Consider the statistics. A check of the beers listed in the rear pages of the 2003 Good Beer Guide shows that out of over 2000 beers listed there are 145 Cask Conditioned Milds, and 60/- Ales in regular production, plus another 22 that are produced seasonally. There are also 18 Low Gravity Bitters. This contrasts with 113 Cask Conditioned Stouts and Porters that are regularly brewed, plus another 75 that are brewed seasonally. However, whilst a lot of Mild is brewed by Regional and some National brewers, most of the Stouts and Porters come from the much smaller micro brewers, so Stout and Porters are in fact much in the minority in terms of barrelage.

It is encouraging to note that more brewers are brewing beers in these styles since LADS was formed, but again the additions are mainly from smaller brewers.

So what is being done to promote these styles of beer? Every year, drinkers are encouraged to Make May a Mild Month. This is supported by activities organised by CAMRA branches, including tastings and trails around pubs selling Milds and 60/- Ales. Brewers and pub chains also lend support. In the last few years, JD Wetherspoon have offered one cask of mild at 99p a pint during the month in most of their pubs.

JOIN CAMRA

If you like good beer and good pubs you could be helping to fight to preserve, protect and promote them. CAMRA was set up in the early seventies to fight against the mass destruction of a part of Britain's heritage.

The giant brewers are still pushing through takeovers, mergers and closures of their smaller regional rivals. They are still trying to impose national brands of beer and lager on their customers whether they like it or not, and they are still closing down town and village pubs or converting them into grotesque 'theme' pubs.

CAMRA wants to see genuine free competition in the brewing industry, fair prices, and, above all, a top quality product brewed by local breweries in accordance with local tastes, and served in pubs that maintain the best features of a tradition that goes back centuries.

As a CAMRA member you will be able to enjoy generous discounts on CAMRA products and receive the highly rated monthly newspaper What's Brewing. You will be given the CAMRA members' handbook and be able to join in local social events and brewery trips.

To join, complete the form below and, if you wish, arrange for direct debit payments by filling in the form overleaf and returning it to CAMRA. To pay by credit card, contact the membership secretary on (01727) 867201.

Full membership £16; Joint (living partners') membership £19; Single under 26, Student, Disabled, Unemployed, Retired over 60 £9; Joint under 26, Joint over 60 £12; UK/EU Life membership £192; UK/EU joint life £228; Single life retired over 60 £90; Joint life retired over 60 £120; Overseas membership £20; Joint overseas £28; Single overseas life £240; Joint overseas life £276.

Please delete as appropriate:

I/We wish to become members of CAMRA.

I/We agree to abide by the memorandum and articles of association of the company.

I/We enclose a cheque/p.o. for £   (payable to CAMRA Ltd.)

Name(s)

Address

Postcode

Signature(s)

CAMRA Ltd., 230 Hatfield Road, St Albans, Herts AL1 4LW

Please fill in the whole form using a ball point pen and send it to:

Campaign for Real Ale Ltd,
230 Hatfield Road,
St. Albans,
Herts
AL1 4LW

Name of Account Holder(s)

Bank/Building Society account number

Branch Sort Code

Name and full postal address of your Bank or Building Society

To The Manager   Bank/Building Society

Address

Postcode

Instruction to your Bank or Building Society to pay by Direct Debit

Originator's Identification Number

| 9 | 2 | 6 | 1 | 2 | 9 |

Reference Number

FOR CAMRA OFFICIAL USE ONLY

This is not part of the instruction to your Bank or Building Society

Membership Number

Name

Postcode

Instructions to your Bank or Building Society
Please pay CAMRA Direct Debits from the account detailed on this instruction subject to the safeguards assured by the Direct Debit Guarantee. I understand that this instruction may remain with CAMRA and, if so, will be passed electronically to my Bank/Building Society

Signature(s)

Date

Banks and Building Societies may not accept Direct Debit instructions for some types of account

---

✂ -

This guarantee should be detached and retained by the Payer.

The
Direct Debit
Guarantee

■ This Guarantee is offered by all Banks and Building Societies that take part in the Direct Debit Scheme. The efficiency and security of the Scheme is monitored and protected by your own Bank or Building Society.

■ If the amounts to be paid or the payment dates change CAMRA will notify you 10 working days in advance of your account being debited or as otherwise agreed.

■ If an error is made by CAMRA or your Bank or Building Society, you are guaranteed a full and immediate refund from your branch of the amount paid.

■ You can cancel a Direct Debit at any time by writing to your Bank or Building Society. Please also send a copy of your letter to us.